A Second Book of Verse by Eugene Field

Eugene Field was born on 2nd September 1850 in St. Louis, Missouri. His mother died when he was six and his father when he was nineteen. His academic life was not taken seriously and he preferred the life of a prankster until, in 1875, he began work as a journalist for the St. Joseph Gazette in Saint Joseph, Missouri.

In his career as a journalist he soon found a niche that suited him. His articles were light, humorous and written in a personal gossipy style that endeared him to his readership. Some were soon being syndicated to other newspapers around the States. Field soon rose to city editor of the Gazette.

Field had first published poetry in 1879, when his poem 'Christmas Treasures' appeared. This was the beginning that would eventually number over a dozen volumes. As well as verse Field published an extensive range of short stories including 'The Holy Cross' and 'Daniel and the Devil.'

In 1889 whilst the family were in London and Field himself was recovering from a bout of ill health he wrote his most famous poem; 'Lovers Lane'.

On 4th November 1895 Eugene Field Sr died in Chicago of a heart attack at the age of 45.

A little bit of a woman came
Athwart my path one day;
So tiny was she that she seemed to be
A pixy strayed from the misty sea,
Or a wandering greenwood fay.

"Oho, you little elf!" I cried,
"And what are you doing here?
So tiny as you will never do
For the brutal rush and hullaballoo
Of this practical world, I fear."

"Voice have I, good sir," said she.—
"'Tis soft as an Angel's sigh,
But to fancy a word of yours were heard
In all the din of this world's absurd!"
Smiling, I made reply.

"Hands have I, good sir" she quoth.—
"Marry, and that have you!
But amid the strife and the tumult rife
In all the struggle and battle for life,
What can those wee hands do?"

"Eyes have I, good sir," she said.—
"Sooth, you have," quoth I,
"And tears shall flow therefrom, I trow,
And they betimes shall dim with woe,
As the hard, hard years go by!"

That little bit of a woman cast
Her two eyes full on me,
And they smote me sore to my inmost core,
And they hold me slaved forevermore,—
Yet would I not be free!

That little bit of a woman's hands
Reached up into my breast
And rent apart my scoffing heart,—
And they buffet it still with such sweet art
As cannot be expressed.

That little bit of a woman's voice
Hath grown most wondrous dear;
Above the blare of all elsewhere
(An inspiration that mocks at care)
It riseth full and clear.

Dear one, I bless the subtle power
That makes me wholly thine;
And I'm proud to say that I bless the day
When a little woman wrought her way
Into this life of mine!

Index of Contents

FATHER'S WAY.

My father was no pessimist; he loved the things of earth,—
Its cheerfulness and sunshine, its music and its mirth.
He never sighed or moped around whenever things went wrong,—
I warrant me he'd mocked at fate with some defiant song;
But, being he warn't much on tune, when times looked sort o' blue,
He'd whistle softly to himself this only tune he knew,—

Now mother, when she heard that tune which father whistled so,
Would say, "There's something wrong to-day with Ephraim, I know;
He never tries to make believe he's happy that 'ere way
But that I'm certain as can be there's somethin' wrong to pay."
And so betimes, quite natural-like, to us observant youth
There seemed suggestion in that tune of deep, pathetic truth.

When Brother William joined the war, a lot of us went down
To see the gallant soldier boys right gayly out of town.
A-comin' home, poor mother cried as if her heart would break,
And all us children, too,—for hers, and not for William's sake!
But father, trudgin' on ahead, his hands behind him so,
Kept whistlin' to himself, so sort of solemn-like and low.

And when my oldest sister, Sue, was married and went West,
Seemed like it took the tuck right out of mother and the rest.
She was the sunlight in our home,—why, father used to say
It wouldn't seem like home at all if Sue should go away;
But when she went, a-leavin' us all sorrer and all tears,
Poor father whistled lonesome-like—and went to feed the steers.

When crops were bad, and other ills befell our homely lot,
He'd set of nights and try to act as if he minded not;
And when came death and bore away the one he worshipped so,
How vainly did his lips belie the heart benumbed with woe!
You see the telltale whistle told a mood he'd not admit,—
He'd always stopped his whistlin' when he thought we noticed it.

I'd like to see that stooping form and hoary head again,—
To see the honest, hearty smile that cheered his fellow-men.
Oh, could I kiss the kindly lips that spake no creature wrong,
And share the rapture of the heart that overflowed with song!
Oh, could I hear the little tune he whistled long ago,
When he did battle with the griefs he would not have us know!

TO MY MOTHER

How fair you are, my mother!
Ah, though 't is many a year
Since you were here,
Still do I see your beauteous face,
And with the glow
Of your dark eyes cometh a grace
Of long ago.
So gentle, too, my mother!
Just as of old, upon my brow,
Like benedictions now,
Falleth your dear hand's touch;
And still, as then,
A voice that glads me over-much
Cometh again,
My fair and gentle mother!

How you have loved me, mother,
I have not power to tell,
Knowing full well
That even in the rest above
It is your will
To watch and guard me with your love,
Loving me still.
And, as of old, my mother,
I am content to be a child,
By mother's love beguiled
From all these other charms;
So to the last
Within thy dear, protecting arms
Hold thou me fast,
My guardian angel, mother!

KÖRNER'S BATTLE PRAYER

Father, I cry to Thee!
Round me the billows of battle are pouring,
Round me the thunders of battle are roaring;
Father on high, hear Thou my cry,—
Father, oh, lead Thou me!

Father, oh, lead Thou me!
Lead me, o'er Death and its terrors victorious,—
See, I acknowledge Thy will as all-glorious;
Point Thou the way, lead where it may,—
God, I acknowledge Thee!

God, I acknowledge Thee!
As when the dead leaves of autumn whirl round me,
So, when the horrors of war would confound me,
Laugh I at fear, knowing Thee near,—
Father, oh, bless Thou me!

Father, oh, bless Thou me!
Living or dying, waking or sleeping,
Such as I am, I commit to Thy keeping:
Frail though I be, Lord, bless Thou me!
Father, I worship Thee!

Father, I worship Thee!
Not for the love of the riches that perish,
But for the freedom and justice we cherish,
Stand we or fall, blessing Thee, all—
God, I submit to Thee!

God, I submit to Thee!
Yea, though the terrors of Death pass before me,
Yea, with the darkness of Death stealing o'er me,
Lord, unto Thee bend I the knee,—
Father, I cry to Thee!

GOSLING STEW

In Oberhausen, on a time,
I fared as might a king;
And now I feel the muse sublime
Inspire me to embalm in rhyme
That succulent and sapid thing
Behight of gentile and of Jew
A gosling stew!

The good Herr Schmitz brought out his best,—
Soup, cutlet, salad, roast,—
And I partook with hearty zest,
And fervently anon I blessed
That generous and benignant host,
When suddenly dawned on my view
A gosling stew!

I sniffed it coming on apace,
And as its odors filled
The curious little dining-place,
I felt a glow suffuse my face,
I felt my very marrow thrilled
With rapture altogether new,—

'Twas gosling stew!

These callow birds had never played
In yonder village pond;
Had never through the gateway strayed,
And plaintive spissant music made
Upon the grassy green beyond:
Cooped up, they simply ate and grew
For gosling stew!

My doctor said I mustn't eat
High food and seasoned game;
But surely gosling is a meat
With tender nourishment replete.
Leastwise I gayly ate this same;
I braved dyspepsy—wouldn't you
For gosling stew?

I've feasted where the possums grow,
Roast turkey have I tried,
The joys of canvasbacks I know,
And frequently I've eaten crow
In bleak and chill Novembertide;
I'd barter all that native crew
For gosling stew!

And when from Rhineland I adjourn
To seek my Yankee shore,
Back shall my memory often turn,
And fiercely shall my palate burn
For sweets I'll taste, alas! no more,—
Oh, that mein kleine frau could brew
A gosling stew!

Vain are these keen regrets of mine,
And vain the song I sing;
Yet would I quaff a stoup of wine
To Oberhausen auf der Rhine,
Where fared I like a very king:
And here's a last and fond adieu
To gosling stew!

CATULLUS TO LESBIA

Come, my Lesbia, no repining;
Let us love while yet we may!
Suns go on forever shining;
But when we have had our day,
Sleep perpetual shall o'ertake us,

And no morrow's dawn awake us.

Come, in yonder nook reclining,
Where the honeysuckle climbs,
Let us mock at Fate's designing,
Let us kiss a thousand times!
And if they shall prove too few, dear,
When they're kissed we'll start anew, dear!

And should any chance to see us,
Goodness! how they'll agonize!
How they'll wish that they could be us,
Kissing in such liberal wise!
Never mind their envious whining;
Come, my Lesbia, no repining!

JOHN SMITH

Today I strayed in Charing Cross, as wretched as could be,
With thinking of my home and friends across the tumbling sea;
There was no water in my eyes, but my spirits were depressed,
And my heart lay like a sodden, soggy doughnut in my breast.
This way and that streamed multitudes, that gayly passed me by;
Not one in all the crowd knew me, and not a one knew I.
"Oh for a touch of home!" I sighed; "oh for a friendly face!
Oh for a hearty hand-clasp in this teeming, desert place!"
And so soliloquizing, as a homesick creature will,
Incontinent, I wandered down the noisy, bustling hill,
And drifted, automatic-like and vaguely, into Lowe's,
Where Fortune had in store a panacea for my woes.
The register was open, and there dawned upon my sight
A name that filled and thrilled me with a cyclone of delight,—
The name that I shall venerate unto my dying day,—
The proud, immortal signature: "John Smith, U. S. A."

Wildly I clutched the register, and brooded on that name;
I knew John Smith, yet could not well identify the same.
I knew him North, I knew him South, I knew him East and West;
I knew him all so well I knew not which I knew the best.
His eyes, I recollect, were gray, and black, and brown, and blue;
And when he was not bald, his hair was of chameleon hue;
Lean, fat, tall, short, rich, poor, grave, gay, a blonde, and a brunette,—
Aha, amid this London fog, John Smith, I see you yet!
I see you yet; and yet the sight is all so blurred I seem
To see you in composite, or as in a waking dream.
Which are you, John? I'd like to know, that I might weave a rhyme
Appropriate to your character, your politics, and clime.
So tell me, were you "raised" or "reared"? your pedigree confess
In some such treacherous ism as "I reckon" or "I guess."

Let fall your telltale dialect, that instantly I may
Identify my countryman, "John Smith, U. S. A."

It's like as not you air the John that lived aspell ago
Deown East, where codfish, beans, 'nd bona-fide schoolma'ams grow;
Where the dear old homestead nestles like among the Hampshire hills,
And where the robin hops about the cherry-boughs 'nd trills;
Where Hubbard squash 'nd huckleberries grow to powerful size,
And everything is orthodox from preachers down to pies;
Where the red-wing blackbirds swing 'nd call beside the pickril pond,
And the crows air cawin' in the pines uv the pasture lot beyond;
Where folks complain uv bein' poor, because their money's lent
Out West on farms 'nd railroads at the rate uv ten per cent;
Where we ust to spark the Baker girls a-comin' home from choir,
Or a-settin' namin' apples round the roarin' kitchen fire;
Where we had to go to meetin' at least three times a week,
And our mothers learnt us good religious Dr. Watts to speak;
And where our grandmas sleep their sleep—God rest their souls, I say;
And God bless yours, ef you're that John, "John Smith, U. S. A."

Or, mebbe, Col. Smith, yo' are the gentleman I know
In the country whar the finest Democrats 'nd hosses grow;
Whar the ladies are all beautiful, an' whar the crap of cawn
Is utilized for Burbon, and true awters are bawn.
You've ren for jedge, and killed yore man, and bet on Proctor Knott;
Yore heart is full of chivalry, yore skin is full of shot;
And I disremember whar I've met with gentlemen so true
As yo' all in Kaintucky, whar blood an' grass are blue,
Whar a niggah with a ballot is the signal fo' a fight,
Whar the yaller dawg pursues the coon throughout the bammy night,
Whar blooms the furtive possum,—pride an' glory of the South!
And anty makes a hoe-cake, sah, that melts within yo' mouth,
Whar all night long the mockin'-birds are warblin' in the trees,
And black-eyed Susans nod and blink at every passing breeze,
Whar in a hallowed soil repose the ashes of our Clay,—
H'yar's lookin' at yo', Col. "John Smith, U. S. A."

Or wuz you that John Smith I knew out yonder in the West,—
That part of our Republic I shall always love the best!
Wuz you him that went prospectin' in the spring of '69
In the Red Hoss Mountain country for the Gosh-all-Hemlock mine?
Oh, how I'd liked to clasped your hand, an' set down by your side,
And talked about the good old days beyond the Big Divide,—
Of the rackaboar, the snaix, the bear, the Rocky Mountain goat,
Of the conversazzhyony, 'nd of Casey's tabble-dote,
And a word of them old pardners that stood by us long ago,—
Three-fingered Hoover, Sorry Tom, and Parson Jim, you know!
Old times, old friends, John Smith, would make our hearts beat high again,
And we'd see the snow-top mountains like we used to see 'em then;
The magpies would go flutterin' like strange sperrits to 'nd fro,
And we'd hear the pines a-singin' in the ragged gulch below;

And the mountain brook would loiter like upon its windin' way,
Ez if it waited for a child to jine it in its play.
You see, John Smith, just which you are I cannot well recall;
And, really, I am pleased to think you somehow must be all!
For when a man sojourns abroad awhile, as I have done,
He likes to think of all the folks he left at home as one.
And so they are,—for well you know there's nothing in a name;
Our Browns, our Joneses, and our Smiths are happily the same,—
All represent the spirit of the land across the sea;
All stand for one high purpose in our country of the free.
Whether John Smith be from the South, the North, the West, the East,
So long as he's American, it mattereth not the least;
Whether his crest be badger, bear, palmetto, sword, or pine,
His is the glory of the stars that with the stripes combine.
Where'er he be, whate'er his lot, he's eager to be known,
Not by his mortal name, but by his country's name alone;
And so, compatriot, I am proud you wrote your name to-day
Upon the register at Lowe's, "John Smith, U. S. A."

ST. MARTIN'S LANE

St. Martin's Lane winds up the hill,
And trends a devious way;
I walk therein amid the din
Of busy London day:
I walk where wealth and squalor meet,
And think upon a time
When others trod this saintly sod,
And heard St. Martin's chime.

But when those solemn bells invoke
The midnight's slumbrous grace,
The ghosts of men come back again
To haunt that curious place:
The ghosts of sages, poets, wits,
Come back in goodly train;
And all night long, with mirth and song,
They walk St. Martin's Lane.

There's Jerrold paired with Thackeray,
Maginn and Thomas Moore,
And here and there and everywhere
Fraserians by the score;
And one wee ghost that climbs the hill
Is welcomed with a shout,—
No king could be revered as he,—
The padre, Father Prout!

They banter up and down the street,

And clamor at the door
Of yonder inn, which once has been
The scene of mirth galore:
'Tis now a lonely, musty shell,
Deserted, like to fall;
And Echo mocks their ghostly knocks,
And iterates their call.

Come back, thou ghost of ruddy host,
From Pluto's misty shore;
Renew to-night the keen delight
Of by-gone years once more;
Brew for this merry, motley horde,
And serve the steaming cheer;
And grant that I may lurk hard by,
To see the mirth, and hear.

Ah, me! I dream what things may seem
To others childish vain,
And yet at night 'tis my delight
To walk St. Martin's Lane;
For, in the light of other days,
I walk with those I love,
And all the time St. Martin's chime
Makes piteous moan above.

THE SINGING IN GOD'S ACRE

Out yonder in the moonlight, wherein God's Acre lies,
Go angels walking to and fro, singing their lullabies.
Their radiant wings are folded, and their eyes are bended low,
As they sing among the beds whereon the flowers delight to grow,—

"Sleep, oh, sleep!
The Shepherd guardeth His sheep.
Fast speedeth the night away,
Soon cometh the glorious day;
Sleep, weary ones, while ye may,—
Sleep, oh, sleep!"

The flowers within God's Acre see that fair and wondrous sight,
And hear the angels singing to the sleepers through the night;
And, lo! throughout the hours of day those gentle flowers prolong
The music of the angels in that tender slumber-song,—

"Sleep, oh, sleep!
The Shepherd loveth His sheep.
He that guardeth His flock the best
Hath folded them to His loving breast;

So sleep ye now, and take your rest,—
Sleep, oh, sleep!"

From angel and from flower the years have learned that soothing song,
And with its heavenly music speed the days and nights along;
So through all time, whose flight the Shepherd's vigils glorify,
God's Acre slumbereth in the grace of that sweet lullaby,—

"Sleep, oh, sleep!
The Shepherd loveth His sheep.
Fast speedeth the night away,
Soon cometh the glorious day;
Sleep, weary ones, while ye may,—
Sleep, oh, sleep!"

DEAR OLD LONDON

When I was broke in London in the fall of '89,
I chanced to spy in Oxford Street this tantalizing sign,—
"A Splendid Horace cheap for Cash!" Of course I had to look
Upon the vaunted bargain, and it was a noble book!
A finer one I've never seen, nor can I hope to see,—
The first edition, richly bound, and clean as clean can be;
And, just to think, for three-pounds-ten I might have had that Pine,
When I was broke in London in the fall of '89!

Down at Noseda's, in the Strand, I found, one fateful day,
A portrait that I pined for as only maniac may,—
A print of Madame Vestris (she flourished years ago,
Was Bartolozzi's daughter and a thoroughbred, you know).
A clean and handsome print it was, and cheap at thirty bob,—
That's what I told the salesman, as I choked a rising sob;
But I hung around Noseda's as it were a holy shrine,
When I was broke in London in the fall of '89.

At Davey's, in Great Russell Street, were autographs galore,
And Mr. Davey used to let me con that precious store.
Sometimes I read what warriors wrote, sometimes a king's command,
But oftener still a poet's verse, writ in a meagre hand.
Lamb, Byron, Addison, and Burns, Pope, Johnson, Swift, and Scott,—
It needed but a paltry sum to comprehend the lot;
Yet, though Friend Davey marked 'em down, what could I but decline?
For I was broke in London in the fall of '89.

Of antique swords and spears I saw a vast and dazzling heap
That Curio Fenton offered me at prices passing cheap;
And, oh, the quaint old bureaus, and the warming-pans of brass,
And the lovely hideous freaks I found in pewter and in glass!
And, oh, the sideboards, candlesticks, the cracked old china plates,

The clocks and spoons from Amsterdam that antedate all dates!
Of such superb monstrosities I found an endless mine
When I was broke in London in the fall of '89.

O ye that hanker after boons that others idle by,—
The battered things that please the soul, though they may vex the eye,—
The silver plate and crockery all sanctified with grime,
The oaken stuff that has defied the tooth of envious Time,
The musty tomes, the speckled prints, the mildewed bills of play,
And other costly relics of malodorous decay,—
Ye only can appreciate what agony was mine
When I was broke in London in the fall of '89.

When, in the course of natural things, I go to my reward,
Let no imposing epitaph my martyrdoms record;
Neither in Hebrew, Latin, Greek, nor any classic tongue,
Let my ten thousand triumphs over human griefs be sung;
But in plain Anglo-Saxon—that he may know who seeks
What agonizing pangs I've had while on the hunt for freaks—
Let there be writ upon the slab that marks my grave this line:
"Deceased was broke in London in the fall of '89."

CORSICAN LULLABY

Bambino in his cradle slept;
And by his side his grandam grim
Bent down and smiled upon the child,
And sung this lullaby to him,—
This "ninna and anninia":

"When thou art older, thou shalt mind
To traverse countries far and wide,
And thou shalt go where roses blow
And balmy waters singing glide—
So ninna and anninia!

"And thou shalt wear, trimmed up in points,
A famous jacket edged in red,
And, more than that, a peaked hat,
All decked in gold, upon thy head—
Ah! ninna and anninia!

"Then shalt thou carry gun and knife.
Nor shall the soldiers bully thee;
Perchance, beset by wrong or debt,
A mighty bandit thou shalt be—
So ninna and anninia!

"No woman yet of our proud race

Lived to her fourteenth year unwed;
The brazen churl that eyed a girl
Bought her the ring or paid his head—
So ninna and anninia!

"But once came spies (I know the thieves!)
And brought disaster to our race;
God heard us when our fifteen men
Were hanged within the market-place—
But ninna and anninia!

"Good men they were, my babe, and true,—
Right worthy fellows all, and strong;
Live thou and be for them and me
Avenger of that deadly wrong—
So ninna and anninia!"

THE CLINK OF THE ICE

Notably fond of music, I dote on a sweeter tone
Than ever the harp has uttered or ever the lute has known.
When I wake at five in the morning with a feeling in my head
Suggestive of mild excesses before I retired to bed;
When a small but fierce volcano vexes me sore inside,
And my throat and mouth are furred with a fur that seemeth a buffalo hide,—
How gracious those dews of solace that over my senses fall
At the clink of the ice in the pitcher the boy brings up the hall!

Oh, is it the gaudy ballet, with features I cannot name,
That kindles in virile bosoms that slow but devouring flame?
Or is it the midnight supper, eaten before we retire,
That presently by combustion setteth us all afire?
Or is it the cheery magnum?—nay, I'll not chide the cup
That makes the meekest mortal anxious to whoop things up:
Yet, what the cause soever, relief comes when we call,—
Relief with that rapturous clinkety-clink that clinketh alike for all.

I've dreamt of the fiery furnace that was one vast bulk of flame,
And that I was Abednego a-wallowing in that same;
And I've dreamt I was a crater, possessed of a mad desire
To vomit molten lava, and to snort big gobs of fire;
I've dreamt I was Roman candles and rockets that fizzed and screamed,—
In short, I have dreamt the cussedest dreams that ever a human dreamed:
But all the red-hot fancies were scattered quick as a wink
When the spirit within that pitcher went clinking its clinkety-clink.

Boy, why so slow in coming with that gracious, saving cup?
Oh, haste thee to the succor of the man who is burning up!
See how the ice bobs up and down, as if it wildly strove

To reach its grace to the wretch who feels like a red-hot kitchen stove!
The piteous clinks it clinks methinks should thrill you through and through:
An erring soul is wanting drink, and he wants it p. d. q.!
And, lo! the honest pitcher, too, falls in so dire a fret
That its pallid form is presently bedewed with a chilly sweat.

May blessings be showered upon the man who first devised this drink
That happens along at five A. M. with its rapturous clinkety-clink!
I never have felt the cooling flood go sizzling down my throat
But what I vowed to hymn a hymn to that clinkety-clink devote;
So now, in the prime of my manhood, I polish this lyric gem
For the uses of all good fellows who are thirsty at five A. M.,
But specially for those fellows who have known the pleasing thrall
Of the clink of the ice in the pitcher the boy brings up the hall.

THE BELLS OF NOTRE DAME

What though the radiant thoroughfare
Teems with a noisy throng?
What though men bandy everywhere
The ribald jest and song?
Over the din of oaths and cries
Broodeth a wondrous calm,
And mid that solemn stillness rise
The bells of Notre Dame.

"Heed not, dear Lord," they seem to say,
"Thy weak and erring child;
And thou, O gentle Mother, pray
That God be reconciled;
And on mankind, O Christ, our King,
Pour out Thy gracious balm,"—
'Tis thus they plead and thus they sing,
Those bells of Notre Dame.

And so, methinks, God, bending down
To ken the things of earth,
Heeds not the mockery of the town
Or cries of ribald mirth;
For ever soundeth in His ears
A penitential psalm,—
'T is thy angelic voice He hears,
O bells of Notre Dame!

Plead on, O bells, that thy sweet voice
May still forever be
An intercession to rejoice
Benign divinity;
And that thy tuneful grace may fall

Like dew, a quickening balm,
Upon the arid hearts of all,
O bells of Notre Dame!

LOVER'S LANE, SAINT JO

Saint Jo, Buchanan County,
Is leagues and leagues away;
And I sit in the gloom of this rented room,
And pine to be there to-day.
Yes, with London fog around me
And the bustling to and fro,
I am fretting to be across the sea
In Lover's Lane, Saint Jo.

I would have a brown-eyed maiden
Go driving once again;
And I'd sing the song, as we snailed along,
That I sung to that maiden then:
I purposely say, "as we snailed along,"
For a proper horse goes slow
In those leafy aisles, where Cupid smiles,
In Lover's Lane, Saint Jo.

From her boudoir in the alders
Would peep a lynx-eyed thrush,
And we'd hear her say, in a furtive way,
To the noisy cricket, "Hush!"
To think that the curious creature
Should crane her neck to know
The various things one says and sings
In Lover's Lane, Saint Jo!

But the maples they should shield us
From the gossips of the place;
Nor should the sun, except by pun,
Profane the maiden's face;
And the girl should do the driving,
For a fellow can't, you know,
Unless he's neglectful of what's quite respectful
In Lover's Lane, Saint Jo.

Ah! sweet the hours of springtime,
When the heart inclines to woo,
And it's deemed all right for the callow wight
To do what he wants to do;
But cruel the age of winter,
When the way of the world says no
To the hoary men who would woo again

In Lover's Lane, Saint Jo!

In the Union Bank of London
Are forty pounds or more,
Which I'm like to spend, ere the month shall end,
In an antiquarian store;
But I'd give it all, and gladly,
If for an hour or so
I could feel the grace of a distant place,—
Of Lover's Lane, Saint Jo.

Let us sit awhile, beloved,
And dream of the good old days,—
Of the kindly shade which the maples made
Round the stanch but squeaky chaise;
With your head upon my shoulder,
And my arm about you so,
Though exiles, we shall seem to be
In Lover's Lane, Saint Jo.

CRUMPETS AND TEA

There are happenings in life that are destined to rise
Like dear, hallowed visions before a man's eyes;
And the passage of years shall not dim in the least
The glory and joy of our Sabbath-day feast,—
The Sabbath-day luncheon that's spread for us three,—
My worthy companions, Teresa and Leigh,
And me, all so hungry for crumpets and tea.

There are cynics who say with invidious zest
That a crumpet's a thing that will never digest;
But I happen to know that a crumpet is prime
For digestion, if only you give it its time.
Or if, by a chance, it should not quite agree,
Why, who would begrudge a physician his fee
For plying his trade upon crumpets and tea?

To toast crumpets quite à la mode, I require
A proper long fork and a proper quick fire;
And when they are browned, without further ado,
I put on the butter, that soaks through and through.
And meantime Teresa, directed by Leigh,
Compounds and pours out a rich brew for us three;
And so we sit down to our crumpets—and tea.

A hand-organ grinds in the street a weird bit,—
Confound those Italians! I wish they would quit
Interrupting our feast with their dolorous airs,

Suggestive of climbing the heavenly stairs.
(It's thoughts of the future, as all will agree,
That we fain would dismiss from our bosoms when we
Sit down to discussion of crumpets and tea!)

The Sabbath-day luncheon whereof I now speak
Quite answers its purpose the rest of the week;
Yet with the next Sabbath I wait for the bell
Announcing the man who has crumpets to sell;
Then I scuttle downstairs in a frenzy of glee,
And purchase for sixpence enough for us three,
Who hunger and hanker for crumpets and tea.

But soon—ah! too soon—I must bid a farewell
To joys that succeed to the sound of that bell,
Must hie me away from the dank, foggy shore
That's filled me with colic and—yearnings for more!
Then the cruel, the heartless, the conscienceless sea
Shall bear me afar from Teresa and Leigh
And the other twin friendships of crumpets and tea.

Yet often, ay, ever, before my wan eyes
That Sabbath-day luncheon of old shall arise.
My stomach, perhaps, shall improve by the change,
Since crumpets it seems to prefer at long range;
But, oh, how my palate will hanker to be
In London again with Teresa and Leigh,
Enjoying the rapture of crumpets and tea!

AN IMITATION OF DR. WATTS

Through all my life the poor shall find
In me a constant friend;
And on the meek of every kind
My mercy shall attend.

The dumb shall never call on me
In vain for kindly aid;
And in my hands the blind shall see
A bounteous alms displayed.

In all their walks the lame shall know
And feel my goodness near;
And on the deaf will I bestow
My gentlest words of cheer.

'Tis by such pious works as these,
Which I delight to do,
That men their fellow-creatures please,

And please their Maker too.

INTRY-MINTRY

Willie and Bess, Georgie and May,—
Once as these children were hard at play,
An old man, hoary and tottering, came
And watched them playing their pretty game.
He seemed to wonder, while standing there,
What the meaning thereof could be.
Aha, but the old man yearned to share
Of the little children's innocent glee,
As they circled around with laugh and shout,
And told this rhyme at counting out:
"Intry-mintry, cutrey-corn,
Apple-seed and apple-thorn,
Wire, brier, limber, lock,
Twelve geese in a flock;
Some flew east, some flew west,
Some flew over the cuckoo's nest."

Willie and Bess, Georgie and May,—
Ah, the mirth of that summer day!
'Twas Father Time who had come to share
The innocent joy of those children there.
He learned betimes the game they played,
And into their sport with them went he,—
How could the children have been afraid,
Since little they recked who he might be?
They laughed to hear old Father Time
Mumbling that curious nonsense rhyme
Of intry-mintry, cutrey-corn,
Apple-seed and apple-thorn,
Wire, brier, limber, lock,
Twelve geese in a flock;
Some flew east, some flew west,
Some flew over the cuckoo's nest.

Willie and Bess, Georgie and May,
And joy of summer,—where are they?
The grim old man still standeth near,
Crooning the song of a far-off year;
And into the winter I come alone,
Cheered by that mournful requiem,
Soothed by the dolorous monotone
That shall count me off as it counted them,—
The solemn voice of old Father Time,
Chanting the homely nursery rhyme
He learned of the children a summer morn,

When, with "apple-seed and apple-thorn,"
Life was full of the dulcet cheer
That bringeth the grace of heaven anear:
The sound of the little ones hard at play,—
Willie and Bess, Georgie and May.

MODJESKY AS CAMEEL

Afore we went to Denver we had heerd the Tabor Grand,
Allowed by critics ez the finest opry in the land;
And, roundin' up at Denver in the fall of '81,
Well heeled in p'int uv looker 'nd a-pinin' for some fun,
We told Bill Bush that we wuz fixed quite comf'table for wealth,
And hadn't struck that altitood entirely for our health.
You see we knew Bill Bush at Central City years ago;
(An' a whiter man than that same Bill you could not wish to know!)
Bill run the Grand for Tabor, 'nd he gin us two a deal
Ez how we really otter see Modjesky ez Cameel.

Three-Fingered Hoover stated that he'd great deal ruther go
To call on Charley Sampson than frequent a opry show.
"The queen uv tradegy," sez he, "is wot I've never seen,
And I reckon there is more for me in some other kind uv queen."
"Git out!" sez Bill, disgusted-like, "and can't you never find
A pleasure in the things uv life wich ellervates the mind?
You've set around in Casey's restawraw a year or more,
An' heerd ol' Vere de Blaw perform shef doovers by the score,
Only to come down here among us tong an' say you feel
You'd ruther take in faro than a opry like 'Cameel'!"

But it seems it wurn't no opry, but a sort uv foreign play,
With a heap uv talk an' dressin' that wuz both dekollytay.
A young chap sparks a gal, who's caught a dook that's old an' wealthy,—
She has a cold 'nd faintin' fits, and is gin'rally onhealthy.
She says she has a record; but the young chap doesn't mind,
And it looks ez if the feller wuz a proper likely kind
Until his old man sneaks around 'nd makes a dirty break,
And the young one plays the sucker 'nd gives the girl the shake.
"Armo! Armo!" she hollers; but he flings her on the floor,
And says he ainter goin' to have no truck with her no more.

At that Three-Fingered Hoover says, "I'll chip into this game,
And see if Red Hoss Mountain cannot reconstruct the same.
I won't set by an' see the feelin's uv a lady hurt,—
Gol durn a critter, anyhow, that does a woman dirt!"
He riz up like a giant in that little painted pen,
And stepped upon the platform with the women-folks 'nd men;
Across the trough of gaslights he bounded like a deer,
An' grabbed Armo an' hove him through the landscape in the rear;

And then we seen him shed his hat an' reverently kneel,
An' put his strong arms tenderly around the gal Cameel.

A-standin' in his stockin' feet, his height wuz six foot three,
And a huskier man than Hoover wuz you could not hope to see.
He downed Lafe Dawson wrasslin'; and one night I seen him lick
Three Cornish miners that come into camp from Roarin' Crick
To clean out Casey's restawraw an' do the town, they said.
He could whip his weight in wildcats, an' paint whole townships red,
But good to helpless folks and weak,—a brave and manly heart
A cyclone couldn't phase, but any child could rend apart;
Jest like the mountain pine, wich dares the storm that howls along,
But rocks the winds uv summer-time, an' sings a soothin' song.

"Cameel," sez he, "your record is ag'in you, I'll allow,
But, bein' you're a woman, you'll git justice anyhow;
So, if you say you're sorry, and intend to travel straight,—
Why, never mind that other chap with which you meant to mate,—
I'll marry you myself, and take you back to-morrow night
To the camp on Red Hoss Mountain, where the boys'll treat you white,
Where Casey runs a tabble dote, and folks are brave 'nd true,
Where there ain't no ancient history to bother me or you,
Where there ain't no law but honesty, no evidence but facts,
Where between the verdick and the rope there ain't no onter acts."

I wuz mighty proud of Hoover; but the folks began to shout
That the feller was intrudin', and would some one put him out.
"Well, no; I reckon not," says I, or words to that effect,
Ez I perduced a argument I thought they might respect,—
A long an' harnsome weepon I'd pre-empted when I come
Out West (its cartridges wuz big an' juicy ez a plum),
Wich, when persented properly, wuz very apt to sway
The popular opinion in a most persuasive way.
"Well, no; I reckon not," says I; but I didn't say no more,
Observin' that there wuz a ginral movement towards the door.

First Dr. Lemen he allowed that he had got to go
And see a patient he jest heerd wuz lyin' very low;
An' Charlie Toll riz up an' said he guessed he'd jine the Dock,
An' go to see a client wich wuz waitin' round the block;
John Arkins reckollected he had interviews to write,
And previous engagements hurried Cooper from our sight;
Cal Cole went out to buy a hoss, Fred Skiff and Belford too;
And Stapleton remembered he had heaps uv work to do.
Somehow or other every one wuz full of business then;
Leastwise, they all vamoosed, and didn't bother us again.

I reckollect that Willard Morse an' Bush come runnin' in,
A-hollerin', "Oh, wot two idiots you durned fools have been!"
I reckollect that they allowed we'd made a big mistake,—
They otter knowed us tenderfoots wuz sure to make a break!

An', while Modjesky stated we wuz somewhat off our base,
I half opined she liked it, by the look upon her face.
I reckollect that Hoover regretted he done wrong
In throwin' that there actor through a vista ten miles long.
I reckollect we all shuck hands, and ordered vin frappay,—
And I never shall forget the head I had on me next day!

I haven't seen Modjesky since; I'm hopin' to again.
She's goin' to show in Denver soon; I'll go to see her then.
An' may be I shall speak to her, wich if I do 'twill be
About the old friend restin' by the mighty Western sea,—
A simple man, perhaps, but good ez gold and true ez steel;
He could whip his weight in wildcats, and you never heerd him squeal;
Good to the helpless and the weak; a brave an' manly heart
A cyclone couldn't phase, but any child could rend apart;
So like the mountain pine, that dares the storm wich sweeps along,
But rocks the winds uv summer-time, an' sings a soothin' song.

TELLING THE BEES

Out of the house where the slumberer lay
Grandfather came one summer day,
And under the pleasant orchard trees
He spake this wise to the murmuring bees:
"The clover-bloom that kissed her feet
And the posie-bed where she used to play
Have honey store, but none so sweet
As ere our little one went away.
O bees, sing soft, and, bees, sing low;
For she is gone who loved you so."

A wonder fell on the listening bees
Under those pleasant orchard trees,
And in their toil that summer day
Ever their murmuring seemed to say:
"Child, O child, the grass is cool,
And the posies are waking to hear the song
Of the bird that swings by the shaded pool,
Waiting for one that tarrieth long."
'Twas so they called to the little one then,
As if to call her back again.

O gentle bees, I have come to say
That grandfather fell asleep to-day,
And we know by the smile on grandfather's face
He has found his dear one's biding-place.
So, bees, sing soft, and, bees, sing low,
As over the honey-fields you sweep,—
To the trees abloom and the flowers ablow

Sing of grandfather fast asleep;
And ever beneath these orchard trees
Find cheer and shelter, gentle bees.

THE TEA-GOWN

My lady has a tea-gown
That is wondrous fair to see,—
It is flounced and ruffed and plaited and puffed,
As a tea-gown ought to be;
And I thought she must be jesting
Last night at supper when
She remarked, by chance, that it came from France,
And had cost but two pounds ten.

Had she told me fifty shillings,
I might (and wouldn't you?)
Have referred to that dress in a way folks express
By an eloquent dash or two;
But the guileful little creature
Knew well her tactics when
She casually said that that dream in red
Had cost but two pounds ten.

Yet our home is all the brighter
For that dainty, sensient thing,
That floats away where it properly may,
And clings where it ought to cling;
And I count myself the luckiest
Of all us married men
That I have a wife whose joy in life
Is a gown at two pounds ten.

It isn't the gown compels me
Condone this venial sin;
It's the pretty face above the lace,
And the gentle heart within.
And with her arms about me
I say, and say again,
"'Twas wondrous cheap,"—and I think a heap
Of that gown at two pounds ten!

DOCTORS

'Tis quite the thing to say and sing
Gross libels on the doctor,—
To picture him an ogre grim

Or humbug-pill concocter;
Yet it's in quite another light
My friendly pen would show him,
Glad that it may with verse repay
Some part of what I owe him.

When one's all right, he's prone to spite
The doctor's peaceful mission;
But when he's sick, it's loud and quick
He bawls for a physician.
With other things, the doctor brings
Sweet babes, our hearts to soften:
Though I have four, I pine for more,—
Good doctor, pray come often!

What though he sees death and disease
Run riot all around him?
Patient and true, and valorous too,
Such have I always found him.
Where'er he goes, he soothes our woes;
And when skill's unavailing,
And death is near, his words of cheer
Support our courage failing.

In ancient days they used to praise
The godlike art of healing,—
An art that then engaged all men
Possessed of sense and feeling.
Why, Raleigh, he was glad to be
Famed for a quack elixir;
And Digby sold, as we are told,
A charm for folk lovesick, sir.

Napoleon knew a thing or two,
And clearly he was partial
To doctors, for in time of war
He chose one for a marshal.
In our great cause a doctor was
The first to pass death's portal,
And Warren's name at once became
A beacon and immortal.

A heap, indeed, of what we read
By doctors is provided;
For to those groves Apollo loves
Their leaning is decided.
Deny who may that Rabelais
Is first in wit and learning,
And yet all smile and marvel while
His brilliant leaves they're turning.

How Lever's pen has charmed all men!
How touching Rab's short story!
And I will stake my all that Drake
Is still the schoolboy's glory.
A doctor-man it was began
Great Britain's great museum,—
The treasures there are all so rare
It drives me wild to see 'em!

There's Cuvier, Parr, and Rush; they are
Big monuments to learning.
To Mitchell's prose (how smooth it flows!)
We all are fondly turning.
Tomes might be writ of that keen wit
Which Abernethy's famed for;
With bread-crumb pills he cured the ills
Most doctors now get blamed for.

In modern times the noble rhymes
Of Holmes, a great physician,
Have solace brought and wisdom taught
To hearts of all condition.
The sailor, bound for Puget Sound,
Finds pleasure still unfailing,
If he but troll the barcarole
Old Osborne wrote on Whaling.

If there were need, I could proceed
Ad naus. with this prescription,
But, inter nos, a larger dose
Might give you fits conniption;
Yet, ere I end, there's one dear friend
I'd hold before these others,
For he and I in years gone by
Have chummed around like brothers.

Together we have sung in glee
The songs old Horace made for
Our genial craft, together quaffed
What bowls that doctor paid for!
I love the rest, but love him best;
And, were not times so pressing,
I'd buy and send—you smile, old friend?
Well, then, here goes my blessing.

BARBARA

Blithe was the youth that summer day,
As he smote at the ribs of earth,

And he plied his pick with a merry click,
And he whistled anon in mirth;
And the constant thought of his dear one's face
Seemed to illumine that ghostly place.

The gaunt earth envied the lover's joy,
And she moved, and closed on his head:
With no one nigh and with never a cry
The beautiful boy lay dead;
And the treasure he sought for his sweetheart fair
Crumbled, and clung to his glorious hair.

Fifty years is a mighty space
In the human toil for bread;
But to Love and to Death 'tis merely a breath,
A dream that is quickly sped,—
Fifty years, and the fair lad lay
Just as he fell that summer day.

At last came others in quest of gold,
And hewed in that mountain place;
And deep in the ground one time they found
The boy with the smiling face:
All uncorrupt by the pitiless air,
He lay, with his crown of golden hair.

They bore him up to the sun again,
And laid him beside the brook,
And the folk came down from the busy town
To wonder and prate and look;
And so, to a world that knew him not,
The boy came back to the old-time spot.

Old Barbara hobbled among the rest,—
Wrinkled and bowed was she,—
And she gave a cry, as she fared anigh,
"At last he is come to me!"
And she kneeled by the side of the dead boy there,
And she kissed his lips, and she stroked his hair.

"Thine eyes are sealed, O dearest one!
And better it is 'tis so,
Else thou mightst see how harsh with me
Dealt Life thou couldst not know:
Kindlier Death has kept thee fair;
The sorrow of Life hath been my share."

Barbara bowed her aged face,
And fell on the breast of her dead;
And the golden hair of her dear one there
Caressed her snow-white head.

Oh, Life is sweet, with its touch of pain;
But sweeter the Death that joined those twain.

THE CAFÉ MOLINEAU

The Café Molineau is where
A dainty little minx
Serves God and man as best she can
By serving meats and drinks.
Oh, such an air the creature has,
And such a pretty face!
I took delight that autumn night
In hanging round the place.

I know but very little French
(I have not long been here);
But when she spoke, her meaning broke
Full sweetly on my ear.
Then, too, she seemed to understand
Whatever I'd to say,
Though most I knew was "oony poo,"
"Bong zhoor," and "see voo play."

The female wit is always quick,
And of all womankind
'Tis here in France that you, perchance,
The keenest wits shall find;
And here you'll find that subtle gift,
That rare, distinctive touch,
Combined with grace of form and face,
That glads men overmuch.

"Our girls at home," I mused aloud,
"Lack either that or this;
They don't combine the arts divine
As does the Gallic miss.
Far be it from me to malign
Our belles across the sea,
And yet I'll swear none can compare
With this ideal She."

And then I praised her dainty foot
In very awful French,
And parleyvood in guileful mood
Until the saucy wench
Tossed back her haughty auburn head,
And froze me with disdain:
"There are on me no flies," said she,
"For I come from Bangor, Maine!"

HOLLY AND IVY

Holy standeth in ye house
When that Noel draweth near;
Evermore at ye door
Standeth Ivy, shivering sore
In ye night wind bleak and drear;
And, as weary hours go by,
Doth ye one to other cry.

"Sister Holly," Ivy quoth,
"What is that within you see?
To and fro doth ye glow
Of ye yule-log flickering go;
Would its warmth did cherish me!
Where thou bidest is it warm;
I am shaken of ye storm."

"Sister Ivy," Holly quoth,
"Brightly burns the yule-log here,
And love brings beauteous things,
While a guardian angel sings
To the babes that slumber near;
But, O Ivy! tell me now,
What without there seest thou?"

"Sister Holly," Ivy quoth,
"With fair music comes ye Morn,
And afar burns ye Star
Where ye wondering shepherds are,
And the Shepherd King is born:
'Peace on earth, good-will to men,'
Angels cry, and cry again."

Holly standeth in ye house
When that Noel draweth near;
Clambering o'er yonder door,
Ivy standeth evermore;
And to them that rightly hear
Each one speaketh of ye love
That outpoureth from Above.

THE BOLTONS, 22

When winter nights are grewsome, and the heavy, yellow fog
Gives to Piccadilly semblance of a dank, malarious bog;

When a demon, with companion in similitude of bell,
Goes round informing people he has crumpets for to sell;
When a weird, asthmatic minstrel haunts your door for hours along,
Until you've paid him tu'pence for the thing he calls a song,—
When, in short, the world's against you, and you'd give that world, and more,
To lay your weary heart at rest upon your native shore,
There's happily one saving thing for you and yours to do:
Go call on Isaac Henderson, The Boltons, 22.

The place is all so cheery and so warm I love to spend
My evenings in communion with the genial host, my friend.
One sees chefs d'œuvre of masters in profusion on the walls,
And a monster canine swaggers up and down the spacious halls;
There are divers things of beauty to astound, instruct, and please,
And everywhere assurance of contentment and of ease:
But best of all the gentle hearts I meet with in the place,—
The host's good-fellowship, his wife's sincere and modest grace;
Why, if there be cordiality that warms you through and through,
It's found at Isaac Henderson's, The Boltons, 22.

My favorite room's the study that is on the second floor;
And there we sit in judgment on men and things galore.
The fire burns briskly in the grate, and sheds a genial glare
On me, who most discreetly have pre-empted Isaac's chair,—
A big, low chair, with grateful springs, and curious device
To keep a fellow's cerebellum comf'table and nice,
A shade obscures the functions of the stately lamp, in spite
Of Mrs. Henderson's demands for somewhat more of light;
But he and I demur, and say a mystic gloom will do
For winter-night communion at The Boltons, 22.

Sometimes he reads me Browning, or from Bryant culls a bit,
And sometimes plucks a gem from Hood's philosophy and wit;
And oftentimes I tell him yarns, and (what I fear is worse)
Recite him sundry specimens of woolly Western verse.
And while his muse and mine transcend the bright Horatian's stars,
He smokes his modest pipe, and I—I smoke his choice cigars!
For best of mild Havanas this considerate host supplies,—
The proper brand, the proper shade, and quite the proper size;
And so I buckle down and smoke and smoke,—and so will you,
If ever you're invited to The Boltons, 22.

But, oh! the best of worldly joys is as a dream short-lived:
'Tis twelve o'clock, and Robinson reports our cab arrived.
A last libation ere we part, and hands all round, and then
A cordial invitation to us both to come again.
So home through Piccadilly and through Oxford Street we jog,
On slippery, noisy pavements and in blinding, choking fog,—
The same old route through Circus, Square, and Quadrant we retrace,
Till we reach the princely mansion known as 20 Alfred Place;
And then we seek our feathery beds of cotton to renew

In dreams the sweet distractions of The Boltons, 22.

God bless you, good friend Isaac, and your lovely, gracious wife;
May health and wealth attend you, and happiness, through life;
And as you sit of evenings that quiet room within,
Know that in spirit I shall be your guest as I have been.
So fill and place beside that chair that dainty claret-cup;
Methinks that ghostly hands shall take the tempting offering up,
That ghostly lips shall touch the bowl and quaff the ruby wine,
Pledging in true affection this toast to thee and thine:
"May God's best blessings fall as falls the gentle, gracious dew
Upon the kindly household at The Boltons, 22!"

DIBDIN'S GHOST

Dear wife, last midnight, whilst I read
The tomes you so despise,
A spectre rose beside the bed,
And spake in this true wise:
"From Canaan's beatific coast
I've come to visit thee,
For I am Frognall Dibdin's ghost,"
Says Dibdin's ghost to me.

I bade him welcome, and we twain
Discussed with buoyant hearts
The various things that appertain
To bibliomaniac arts.
"Since you are fresh from t' other side,
Pray tell me of that host
That treasured books before they died,"
Says I to Dibdin's ghost.

"They've entered into perfect rest;
For in the life they've won
There are no auctions to molest,
No creditors to dun.
Their heavenly rapture has no bounds
Beside that jasper sea;
It is a joy unknown to Lowndes,"
Says Dibdin's ghost to me.

Much I rejoiced to hear him speak
Of biblio-bliss above,
For I am one of those who seek
What bibliomaniacs love.
"But tell me, for I long to hear
What doth concern me most,
Are wives admitted to that sphere?"

Says I to Dibdin's ghost.

"The women folk are few up there;
For 'twere not fair, you know,
That they our heavenly joy should share
Who vex us here below.
The few are those who have been kind
To husbands such as we;
They knew our fads, and didn't mind,"
Says Dibdin's ghost to me.

"But what of those who scold at us
When we would read in bed?
Or, wanting victuals, make a fuss
If we buy books instead?
And what of those who've dusted not
Our motley pride and boast,—
Shall they profane that sacred spot?"
Says I to Dibdin's ghost.

"Oh, no! they tread that other path,
Which leads where torments roll,
And worms, yes, bookworms, vent their wrath
Upon the guilty soul.
Untouched of bibliomaniac grace,
That saveth such as we,
They wallow in that dreadful place,"
Says Dibdin's ghost to me.

"To my dear wife will I recite
What things I've heard you say;
She'll let me read the books by night
She's let me buy by day.
For we together by and by
Would join that heavenly host;
She's earned a rest as well as I,"
Says I to Dibdin's ghost.

THE HAWTHORNE CHILDREN

The Hawthorne children, seven in all,
Are famous friends of mine;
And with what pleasure I recall
How, years ago, one gloomy fall
I took a tedious railway line,
And journeyed by slow stages down
Unto that soporiferous town
(Albeit one worth seeing)
Where Hildegarde, John, Henry, Fred,

And Beatrix and Gwendolen,
And she that was the baby then,—
These famous seven, as aforesaid,
Lived, moved, and had their being.

The Hawthorne children gave me such
A welcome by the sea
That the eight of us were soon in touch,
And, though their mother marvelled much,
Happy as larks were we.
Egad, I was a boy again
With Henry, John, and Gwendolen;
And oh the funny capers
I cut with Hildegarde and Fred!
And oh the pranks we children played;
And oh the deafening noise we made—
'Twould shock my family if they read
About it in the papers!

The Hawthorne children all were smart:
The girls, as I recall,
Had comprehended every art
Appealing to the head and heart;
The boys were gifted, all.
'Twas Hildegarde who showed me how
To hitch a horse and milk a cow
And cook the best of suppers;
With Beatrix upon the sands
I sprinted daily, and was beat;
'Twas Henry trained me to the feat
Of walking round upon my hands
Instead of on my uppers.

The Hawthorne children liked me best
Of evenings, after tea,
For then, by general request,
I spun them yarns about the West,—
Yarns all involving Me!
I represented how I'd slain
The bison on his native plain;
And divers tales of wonder
I told of how I'd fought and bled
In Indian scrimmages galore,
Till Mrs. Hawthorne quoth, "No more,"
And packed her darlings off to bed,
To dream of blood and thunder.

They must have changed a deal since then;
The misses, tall and fair,
And those three handsome, lusty men,—
Would they be girls and boys again,

Were I to happen there,
Down in that spot beside the sea
Where we made such tumultuous glee
That dull autumnal weather?
Ah, me! the years go swiftly by;
And yet how fondly I recall
The week when we were children all,
Dear Hawthorne children, you and I,
Just eight of us together!

THE BOTTLE AND THE BIRD

Once on a time a friend of mine prevailed on me to go
To see the dazzling splendors of a sinful ballet show;
And after we had revelled in the saltatory sights,
We sought a neighboring café for more tangible delights.
When I demanded of my friend what viands he preferred,
He quoth: "A large cold bottle, and a small hot bird!"

Fool that I was, I did not know what anguish hidden lies
Within the morceau that allures the nostrils and the eyes!
There is a glorious candor in an honest quart of wine,
A certain inspiration which I cannot well define!
How it bubbles, how it sparkles, how its gurgling seems to say:
"Come! on a tide of rapture let me float your soul away!"

But the crispy, steaming mouthful that is spread upon your plate,—
How it discounts human sapience and satirizes fate!
You wouldn't think a thing so small could cause the pains and aches
That certainly accrue to him that of that thing partakes;
To me, at least, (a guileless wight!) it never once occurred
What horror was encompassed in that small hot bird.

Oh, what a head I had on me when I awoke next day,
And what a firm conviction of intestinal decay!
What seas of mineral water and of bromide I applied
To quench those fierce volcanic fires that rioted inside!
And oh the thousand solemn, awful vows I plighted then
Never to tax my system with a small hot bird again!

The doctor seemed to doubt that birds could worry people so,
But, bless him! since I ate the bird, I guess I ought to know!
The acidous condition of my stomach, so he said,
Bespoke a vinous irritant that amplified my head,
And, ergo, the causation of the thing, as he inferred,
Was the large cold bottle,—not the small hot bird.

Of course I know it wasn't, and I'm sure you'll say I'm right
If ever it has been your wont to train around at night.

How sweet is retrospection when one's heart is bathed in wine,
And before its balmy breath how do the ills of life decline!
How the gracious juices drown what griefs would vex a mortal breast,
And float the flattered soul into the port of dreamless rest!

But you, O noxious, pygmy bird! whether it be you fly,
Or paddle in the stagnant pools that sweltering festering lie,—
I curse you and your evil kind for that you do me wrong,
Engendering poisons that corrupt my petted muse of song;
Go, get thee hence! and never more discomfit me and mine,—
I fain would barter all thy brood for one sweet draught of wine!

So hither come, O sportive youth! when fades the telltale day,—
Come hither, with your fillets and your wreaths of posies gay;
We shall unloose the fragrant seas of seething, frothing wine
Which now the cobwebbed glass and envious wire and corks confine,
And midst the pleasing revelry the praises shall be heard
Of the large cold bottle,—not the small hot bird!

AN ECLOGUE FROM VIRGIL

[The exile Melibœus finds Tityrus in possession of his own farm, restored to him by the Emperor Augustus, and a conversation ensues. The poem is in praise of Augustus, peace, and pastoral life.]

MELIBŒUS
Tityrus, all in the shade of the wide-spreading beech-tree reclining,
Sweet is that music you've made on your pipe that is oaten and slender;
Exiles from home, you beguile our hearts from their hopeless repining,
As you sing Amaryllis the while in pastorals tuneful and tender.

TITYRUS
A god—yes, a god, I declare—vouchsafes me these pleasant conditions,
And often I gayly repair with a tender white lamb to his altar;
He gives me the leisure to play my greatly admired compositions,
While my heifers go browsing all day, unhampered of bell and of halter.

MELIBŒUS
I do not begrudge you repose; I simply admit I'm confounded
To find you unscathed of the woes of pillage and tumult and battle.
To exile and hardship devote, and by merciless enemies hounded,
I drag at this wretched old goat and coax on my famishing cattle.
Oh, often the omens presaged the horrors which now overwhelm me—
But, come, if not elsewise engaged, who is this good deity, tell me!

TITYRUS (reminiscently)
The city—the city called Rome, with my head full of herding and tillage,
I used to compare with my home, these pastures wherein you now wander;
But I didn't take long to find out that the city surpasses the village
As the cypress surpasses the sprout that thrives in the thicket out yonder.

MELIBŒUS

Tell me, good gossip, I pray, what led you to visit the city?

TITYRUS

Liberty! which on a day regarded my lot with compassion;
My age and distresses, forsooth, compelled that proud mistress to pity,
That had snubbed the attentions of youth in most reprehensible fashion.
Oh, happy, thrice happy, the day when the cold Galatea forsook me;
And equally happy, I say, the hour when that other girl took me!

MELIBŒUS (slyly, as if addressing the damsel)

So now, Amaryllis, the truth of your ill-disguised grief I discover!
You pined for a favorite youth with cityfied damsels hobnobbing;
And soon your surroundings partook of your grief for your recusant lover,—
The pine-trees, the copse and the brook, for Tityrus ever went sobbing.

TITYRUS

Melibœus, what else could I do? Fate doled me no morsel of pity;
My toil was all vain the year through, no matter how earnest or clever,
Till, at last, came that god among men, that king from that wonderful city,
And quoth: "Take your homesteads again; they are yours and your assigns forever!"

MELIBŒUS

Happy, oh, happy old man! rich in what 's better than money,—
Rich in contentment, you can gather sweet peace by mere listening;
Bees with soft murmurings go hither and thither for honey,
Cattle all gratefully low in pastures where fountains are glistening—
Hark! in the shade of that rock the pruner with singing rejoices,—
The dove in the elm and the flock of wood-pigeons hoarsely repining,
The plash of the sacred cascade,—ah, restful, indeed, are these voices,
Tityrus, all in the shade of your wide-spreading beech-tree reclining!

TITYRUS

And he who insures this to me—oh, craven I were not to love him!
Nay, rather the fish of the sea shall vacate the water they swim in,
The stag quit his bountiful grove to graze in the ether above him,
While folk antipodean rove along with their children and women!

MELIBŒUS (suddenly recalling his own misery)

But we who are exiled must go; and whither—ah, whither—God knoweth!
Some into those regions of snow or of desert where Death reigneth only;
Some off to the country of Crete, where rapid Oaxes down floweth;
And desperate others retreat to Britain, the bleak isle and lonely.
Dear land of my birth! shall I see the horde of invaders oppress thee?
Shall the wealth that outspringeth from thee by the hand of the alien be squandered?
Dear cottage wherein I was born! shall another in conquest possess thee,
Another demolish in scorn the fields and the groves where I've wandered?
My flock! nevermore shall you graze on that furze-covered hillside above me;
Gone, gone are the halcyon days when my reed piped defiance to sorrow!
Nevermore in the vine-covered grot shall I sing of the loved ones that love me,—

Let yesterday's peace be forgot in dread of the stormy to-morrow!

TITYRUS
But rest you this night with me here; my bed,—we will share it together,
As soon as you've tasted my cheer, my apples and chestnuts and cheeses;
The evening already is nigh,—the shadows creep over the heather,
And the smoke is rocked up to the sky to the lullaby song of the breezes.

PITTYPAT AND TIPPYTOE

All day long they come and go,—
Pittypat and Tippytoe;
Footprints up and down the hall,
Playthings scattered on the floor,
Finger-marks along the wall,
Tell-tale streaks upon the door,—
By these presents you shall know
Pittypat and Tippytoe.

How they riot at their play!
And, a dozen times a day,
In they troop, demanding bread,—
Only buttered bread will do,
And that butter must be spread
Inches thick with sugar too!
Never yet have I said, "No,
Pittypat and Tippytoe!"

Sometimes there are griefs to soothe,
Sometimes ruffled brows to smooth;
For—I much regret to say—
Tippytoe and Pittypat
Sometimes interrupt their play
With an internecine spat;
Fie! oh, fie! to quarrel so,
Pittypat and Tippytoe!

Oh, the thousand worrying things
Every day recurrent brings!
Hands to scrub and hair to brush,
Search for playthings gone amiss,
Many a murmuring to hush,
Many a little bump to kiss;
Life's indeed a fleeting show,
Pittypat and Tippytoe!

And when day is at an end,
There are little duds to mend;
Little frocks are strangely torn,

Little shoes great holes reveal,
Little hose, but one day worn,
Rudely yawn at toe or heel!
Who but you could work such woe,
Pittypat and Tippytoe!

But when comes this thought to me,
"Some there are that childless be,"
Stealing to their little beds,
With a love I cannot speak,
Tenderly I stroke their heads,
Fondly kiss each velvet cheek.
God help those who do not know
A Pittypat or Tippytoe!

On the floor, along the hall,
Rudely traced upon the wall,
There are proofs in every kind
Of the havoc they have wrought;
And upon my heart you'd find
Just such trademarks, if you sought.
Oh, how glad I am 'tis so,
Pittypat and Tippytoe!

ASHES ON THE SLIDE

When Jim and Bill and I were boys a many years ago.
How gayly did we use to hail the coming of the snow!
Our sleds, fresh painted red and with their runners round and bright,
Seemed to respond right briskly to our clamor of delight
As we dragged them up the slippery road that climbed the rugged hill
Where perched the old frame meetin'-house, so solemn-like and still.

Ah, coasting in those days—those good old days—was fun indeed!
Sleds at that time I'd have you know were paragons of speed!
And if the hill got bare in spots, as hills will do, why then
We'd haul on ice and snow to patch those bald spots up again;
But, oh! with what sad certainty our spirits would subside
When Deacon Frisbee sprinkled ashes where we used to slide!

The deacon he would roll his eyes and gnash his toothless gums,
And clear his skinny throat, and twirl his saintly, bony thumbs,
And tell you: "When I wuz a boy, they taught me to eschew
The godless, ribald vanities which modern youth pursue!
The pathway that leads down to hell is slippery, straight, and wide;
And Satan lurks for prey where little boys are wont to slide!"

Now, he who ever in his life has been a little boy
Will not reprove me when he hears the language I employ

To stigmatize as wickedness the deacon's zealous spite
In interfering with the play wherein we found delight;
And so I say, with confidence, not unalloyed of pride:
"Gol durn the man who sprinkles ashes where the youngsters slide!"

But Deacon Frisbee long ago went to his lasting rest,
His money well invested in farm mortgages out West;
Bill, Jim, and I, no longer boys, have learned through years of strife
That the troubles of the little boy pursue the man through life;
That here and there along the course wherein we hoped to glide
Some envious hand has sprinkled ashes just to spoil our slide!

And that malicious, envious hand is not the deacon's now.
Grim, ruthless Fate, that evil sprite none other is than thou!
Riches and honors, peace and care come at thy beck and go;
The soul, elate with joy to-day, to-morrow writhes in woe;
And till a man has turned his face unto the wall and died,
He must expect to get his share of ashes on his slide!

THE LOST CUPID OF MOSCHUS

"Cupid!" Venus went a-crying;
"Cupid, whither dost thou stray?
Tell me, people, hither hieing,
Have you seen my runaway?
Speak,—my kiss shall be your pay!
Yes, and sweets more gratifying,
If you bring him back to-day.

"Cupid," Venus went a-calling,
"Is a rosy little youth,
But his beauty is inthralling.
He will speak you fair, in sooth,
Wheedle you with glib untruth,—
Honey-like his words; but galling
Are his deeds, and full of ruth!

"Cupid's hair is curling yellow,
And he hath a saucy face;
With his chubby hands the fellow
Shooteth into farthest space,
Heedless of all time and place;
King and squire and punchinello
He delighteth to abase!

"Nude and winged the prankish blade is,
And he speedeth everywhere,
Vexing gentlemen and ladies,
Callow youths and damsels fair

Whom he catcheth unaware,—
Venturing even into Hades,
He hath sown his torments there!

"For that bow, that bow and quiver,—
Oh, they are a cruel twain!
Thinking of them makes me shiver.
Oft, with all his might and main,
Cupid sends those darts profane
Whizzing through my heart and liver,
Setting fire to every vein!

"And the torch he carries blazing,—
Truly 'tis a tiny one;
Yet, that tiny torch upraising,
Cupid scarifies the sun!
Ah, good people, there is none
Knows what mischief most amazing
Cupid's evil torch hath done!

"Show no mercy when you find him!
Spite of every specious plea
And of all his whimpering, bind him!
Full of flatteries is he;
Armed with treachery, cap-a-pie,
He'll play 'possum; never mind him,—
March him straightway back to me!

"Bow and arrows and sweet kisses
He will offer you, no doubt;
But beware those proffered blisses,—
They are venomous throughout!
Seize and bind him fast about;
Mind you,—most important this is:
Bind him, bring him, but—watch out!"

CHRISTMAS EVE

Oh, hush thee, little Dear-my-Soul,
The evening shades are falling,—
Hush thee, my dear, dost thou not hear
The voice of the Master calling?

Deep lies the snow upon the earth,
But all the sky is ringing
With joyous song, and all night long
The stars shall dance, with singing.

Oh, hush thee, little Dear-my-Soul,

And close thine eyes in dreaming,
And angels fair shall lead thee where
The singing stars are beaming.

A shepherd calls his little lambs,
And he longeth to caress them;
He bids them rest upon his breast,
That his tender love may bless them.

So, hush thee, little Dear-my-Soul,
Whilst evening shades are falling,
And above the song of the heavenly throng
Thou shalt hear the Master calling.

CARLSBAD

Dear Palmer, just a year ago we did the Carlsbad cure,
Which, though it be exceeding slow, is as exceeding sure;
To corpulency you were prone, dyspepsia bothered me,—
You tipped the beam at twenty stone and I at ten stone three!
The cure, they told us, works both ways: it makes the fat man lean;
The thin man, after many days, achieves a portly mien;
And though it's true you still are fat, while I am like a crow,—
All skin and feathers,—what of that? The cure takes time, you know.

The Carlsbad scenery is sublime,—that's what the guide-books say;
We did not think so at that time, nor think I so to-day!
The bluffs that squeeze the panting town permit no pleasing views,
But weigh the mortal spirits down and give a chap the blues.
With nothing to amuse us then or mitigate our spleen,
We rose and went to bed again, with three bad meals between;
And constantly we made our moan,—ah, none so drear as we,
When you were weighing twenty stone and I but ten stone three!

We never scaled the mountain-side, for walking was my bane,
And you were much too big to ride the mules that there obtain;
And so we loitered in the shade with Israel out in force,
Or through the Pupp'sche allee strayed and heard the band discourse.
Sometimes it pleased us to recline upon the Tepl's brink,
Or watch the bilious human line file round to get a drink;
Anon the portier's piping tone embittered you and me,
When you were weighing twenty stone and I but ten stone three!

And oh! those awful things to eat! No pudding, cake, or pie,
But just a little dab of meat, and crusts absurdly dry;
Then, too, that water twice a day,—one swallow was enough
To take one's appetite away,—the tepid, awful stuff!
Tortured by hunger's cruel stings, I'd little else to do
Than feast my eyes upon the things prescribed and cooked for you.

The goodies went to you alone, the husks all fell to me,
When you were weighing twenty stone and I weighed ten stone three.

Yet happy days! and rapturous ills! and sweetly dismal date!
When, sandwiched in between those hills, we twain bemoaned our fate.
The little woes we suffered then like mists have sped away,
And I were glad to share again those ills with you to-day,—
To flounder in those rains of June that flood that Austrian vale,
To quaff that tepid Kaiserbrunn and starve on victuals stale!
And often, leagues and leagues away from where we suffered then,
With envious yearnings I survey what cannot be again!

And often in my quiet home, through dim and misty eyes,
I seem to see that curhaus dome blink at the radiant skies;
I seem to hear that Wiener band above the Tepl's roar,—
To feel the pressure of your hand and hear your voice once more;
And, better yet, my heart is warm with thoughts of you and yours,
For friendship hath a sweeter charm than thrice ten thousand cures!
So I am happy to have known that time across the sea
When you were weighing twenty stone and I weighed ten stone three.

THE SUGAR-PLUM TREE

Have you ever heard of the Sugar-Plum Tree?
'Tis a marvel of great renown!
It blooms on the shore of the Lollipop Sea
In the garden of Shut-Eye Town;
The fruit that it bears is so wondrously sweet
(As those who have tasted it say)
That good little children have only to eat
Of that fruit to be happy next day.

When you've got to the tree, you would have a hard time
To capture the fruit which I sing;
The tree is so tall that no person could climb
To the boughs where the sugar-plums swing!
But up in that tree sits a chocolate cat,
And a gingerbread dog prowls below;
And this is the way you contrive to get at
Those sugar-plums tempting you so:

You say but the word to that gingerbread dog,
And he barks with such terrible zest
That the chocolate cat is at once all agog,
As her swelling proportions attest.
And the chocolate cat goes cavorting around
From this leafy limb unto that,
And the sugar-plums tumble, of course, to the ground,—
Hurrah for that chocolate cat!

There are marshmallows, gum-drops, and peppermint canes,
With stripings of scarlet or gold,
And you carry away of the treasure that rains
As much as your apron can hold!
So come, little child, cuddle closer to me
In your dainty white nightcap and gown,
And I'll rock you away to that Sugar-Plum Tree
In the garden of Shut-Eye Town.

RED

Any color, so long as it's red,
Is the color that suits me best,
Though I will allow there is much to be said
For yellow and green and the rest;
But the feeble tints which some affect
In the things they make or buy
Have never—I say it with all respect—
Appealed to my critical eye.

There's that in red that warmeth the blood,
And quickeneth a man within,
And bringeth to speedy and perfect bud
The germs of original sin;
So, though I'm properly born and bred,
I'll own, with a certain zest,
That any color, so long as it's red,
Is the color that suits me best.

For where is a color that can compare
With the blush of a buxom lass;
Or where such warmth as of the hair
Of the genuine white horse class?
And, lo! reflected within this cup
Of cheery Bordeaux I see
What inspiration girdeth me up,—
Yes, red is the color for me!

Through acres and acres of art I've strayed
In Italy, Germany, France;
On many a picture a master has made
I've squandered a passing glance:
Marines I hate, madonnas and
Those Dutch freaks I detest;
But the peerless daubs of my native land,—
They're red, and I like them best.

'Tis little I care how folk deride,—

I'm backed by the West, at least;
And we are free to say that we can't abide
The tastes that obtain down East;
And we're mighty proud to have it said
That here in the versatile West
Most any color, so long as it's red,
Is the color that suits us best.

JEWISH LULLABY

My harp is on the willow-tree,
Else would I sing, O love, to thee
A song of long ago,—
Perchance the song that Miriam sung
Ere yet Judæa's heart was wrung
By centuries of woe.

The shadow of those centuries lies
Deep in thy dark and mournful eyes;
But, hush! and close them now,
And in the dreams that thou shalt dream
The light of other days shall seem
To glorify thy brow.

I ate my crust in tears to-day,
As, scourged, I went upon my way,
And yet my darling smiled,—
Ay, beating at my breast, he laughed;
My anguish curdled not the draught,
'Twas sweet with love, my child.

Our harp is on the willow-tree:
I have no song to sing to thee,
As shadows round us roll;
But, hush! and sleep, and thou shalt hear
Jehovah's voice that speaks to cheer
Judæa's fainting soul.

AT CHEYENNE

Young Lochinvar came in from the west,
With fringe on his trousers and fur on his vest;
The width of his hat brim could nowhere be beat,
His No. 10 brogans were chock full of feet,
His girdle was horrent with pistols and things,
And he nourished a handful of aces on kings.

The fair Mariana sate watching a star,
When who should turn up but the young Lochinvar!
Her pulchritude gave him a pectoral glow,
And he reined up his hoss with stentorian "Whoa!"
Then turned on the maiden a rapturous grin,
And modestly asked if he mightn't step in.

With presence of mind that was marvellous quite,
The fair Mariana replied that he might;
So in through the portal rode young Lochinvar,
Pre-empted the claim, and cleaned out the bar.
Though the justice allowed he wa'n't wholly to blame,
He taxed him ten dollars and costs, just the same.

THE NAUGHTY DOLL

My dolly is a dreadful care,—
Her name is Miss Amandy;
I dress her up and curl her hair,
And feed her taffy candy.
Yet, heedless of the pleading voice
Of her devoted mother,
She will not wed her mother's choice,
But says she'll wed another.

I'd have her wed the china vase,—
There is no Dresden rarer;
You might go searching every place
And never find a fairer.
He is a gentle, pinkish youth,—
Of that there's no denying;
Yet when I speak of him, forsooth!
Amandy falls to crying.

She loves the drum,—that's very plain,—
And scorns the vase so clever,
And, weeping, vows she will remain
A spinster doll forever!
The protestations of the drum
I am convinced are hollow;
When once distressing times should come
How soon would ruin follow!

Yet all in vain the Dresden boy
From yonder mantel woos her;
A mania for that vulgar toy,
The noisy drum, imbues her.
In vain I wheel her to and fro,
And reason with her mildly:

Her waxen tears in torrents flow,
Her sawdust heart beats wildly.

I'm sure that when I'm big and tall,
And wear long trailing dresses,
I sha'n't encourage beaux at all
Till mamma acquiesces;
Our choice will be a suitor then
As pretty as this vase is,—
Oh, how we'll hate the noisy men
With whiskers on their faces!

THE PNEUMOGASTRIC NERVE

Upon an average, twice a week,
When anguish clouds my brow,
My good physician friend I seek
To know "what ails me now."
He taps me on the back and chest,
And scans my tongue for bile,
And lays an ear against my breast
And listens there awhile;
Then is he ready to admit
That all he can observe
Is something wrong inside, to wit:
My pneumogastric nerve!

Now, when these Latin names within
Dyspeptic hulks like mine
Go wrong, a fellow should begin
To draw what's called the line.
It seems, however, that this same,
Which in my hulk abounds,
Is not, despite its awful name,
So fatal as it sounds;
Yet of all torments known to me,
I'll say without reserve,
There is no torment like to thee,
Thou pneumogastric nerve!

This subtle, envious nerve appears
To be a patient foe,—
It waited nearly forty years
Its chance to lay me low;
Then, like some blithering blast of hell,
It struck this guileless bard,
And in that evil hour I fell
Prodigious far and hard.
Alas! what things I dearly love—

Pies, puddings, and preserves—
Are sure to rouse the vengeance of
All pneumogastric nerves!

Oh that I could remodel man!
I'd end these cruel pains
By hitting on a different plan
From that which now obtains.
The stomach, greatly amplified,
Anon should occupy
The all of that domain inside
Where heart and lungs now lie.
But, first of all, I should depose
That diabolic curve
And author of my thousand woes,
The pneumogastric nerve!

TEENY-WEENY

Every evening, after tea,
Teeny-Weeny comes to me,
And, astride my willing knee,
Plies his lash and rides away;
Though that palfrey, all too spare,
Finds his burden hard to bear,
Teeny-Weeny doesn't care,—
He commands, and I obey!

First it's trot; and gallop then,—
Now it's back to trot again;
Teeny-Weeny likes it when
He is riding fierce and fast!
Then his dark eyes brighter grow
And his cheeks are all aglow,—
"More!" he cries, and never "Whoa!"
Till the horse breaks down at last!

Oh, the strange and lovely sights
Teeny-Weeny sees of nights,
As he makes those famous flights
On that wondrous horse of his!
Oftentimes, before he knows,
Wearylike his eyelids close,
And, still smiling, off he goes
Where the land of By-low is.

There he sees the folk of fay
Hard at ring-a-rosie play,
And he hears those fairies say,

"Come, let's chase him to and fro!"
But, with a defiant shout,
Teeny puts that host to rout,—
Of this tale I make no doubt,—
Every night he tells it so!

So I feel a tender pride
In my boy who dares to ride
(That fierce horse of his astride)
Off into those misty lands;
And as on my breast he lies,
Dreaming in that wondrous wise,
I caress his folded eyes,—
Pat his little dimpled hands.

On a time he went away,
Just a little while to stay,
And I'm not ashamed to say
I was very lonely then;
Life without him was so sad,
You can fancy I was glad
And made merry when I had
Teeny-Weeny back again!

So of evenings, after tea,
When he toddles up to me
And goes tugging at my knee,
You should hear his palfrey neigh!
You should see him prance and shy,
When, with an exulting cry,
Teeny-Weeny, vaulting high,
Plies his lash and rides away!

TELKA

Through those golden summer days
Our twin flocks were wont to graze
On the hillside, which the sun
Rested lovingly upon,—
Telka's flock and mine; and we
Sung our songs in rapturous glee,
Idling in the pleasant shade
Which the solemn Yew-tree made,
While the Brook anear us played,
And a white Rose, ghost-like, grew
In the shadow of the Yew.

Telka loved me passing well;
How I loved her none can tell!

How I love her none may know,—
Oh that man love woman so!
When she was not at my side,
Loud my heart in anguish cried,
And my lips, till she replied.
Yet they think to silence me,—
As if love could silenced be!
Fool were I, and fools were they!
Still I wend my lonely way,
"Telka," evermore I cry;
Answer me the woods and sky,
And the weary years go by.

Telka, she was passing fair;
And the glory of her hair
Was such glory as the sun
With his blessing casts upon
Yonder lonely mountain height,
Lifting up to bid good-night
To her sovereign in the west,
Sinking wearily to rest,
Drowsing in that golden sea
Where the realms of Dreamland be.

So our love to fulness grew,
Whilst beneath the solemn Yew
Ghost-like paled the Rose of white,
As it were some fancied sight
Blanched it with a dread affright.

Telka, she was passing fair;
And our peace was perfect there
Till, enchanted by her smile,
Lurked the South Wind there awhile,
Underneath that hillside tree
Where with singing idled we,
And I heard the South Wind say
Flattering words to her that day
Of a city far away.
But the Yew-tree crouched as though
It were like to whisper No
To the words the South Wind said
As he smoothed my Telka's head.
And the Brook, all pleading, cried
To the dear one at my side:
"Linger always where I am;
Stray not thence, O cosset lamb!
Wander not where shadows deep
On the treacherous quicksands sleep,
And the haunted waters leap;
Be thou ware the waves that flow

Toward the prison pool below,
Where, beguiled from yonder sky,
Captive moonbeams shivering lie,
And at dawn of morrow die."
So the Brook to Telka cried,
But my Telka naught replied;
And, as in a strange affright,
Paled the Rose a ghostlier white.

When anon the North Wind came,—
Rudely blustering Telka's name,
And he kissed the leaves that grew
Round about the trembling Yew,—
Kissed and romped till, blushing red,
All one day in terror fled,
And the white Rose hung her head;
Coming to our trysting spot,
Long I called; she answered not.
"Telka!" pleadingly I cried
Up and down the mountain-side
Where we twain were wont to bide.

There were those who thought that I
Could be silenced with a lie,
And they told me Telka's name
Should be spoken now with shame:
"She is lost to us and thee,"—
That is what they said to me.

"Is my Telka lost?" quoth I.
"On this hilltop shall I cry,
So that she may hear and then
Find her way to me again.
The South Wind spoke a lie that day;
All deceived, she lost her way
Yonder where the shadows sleep
'Mongst the haunted waves that leap
Over treacherous quicksands deep,
And where captive moonbeams lie
Doomed at morrow's dawn to die
She is lost, and that is all;
I will search for her, and call."

Summer comes and winter goes,
Buds the Yew and blooms the Rose;
All the others are anear,—
Only Telka is not here!
Gone the peace and love I knew
Sometime 'neath the hillside Yew;
And the Rose, that mocks me so,
I had crushed it long ago

But that Telka loved it then,
And shall soothe its terror when
She comes back to me again.
Call I, seek I everywhere
For my Telka, passing fair.
It is, oh, so many a year
I have called! She does not hear,
Yet nor feared nor worn am I;
For I know that if I cry
She shall sometime hear my call.
She is lost, and that is all,—
She is lost in some far spot;
I have searched, and found it not.
Could she hear me calling, then
Would she come to me again;
For she loved me passing well,—
How I love her none can tell!
That is why these years I've cried
"Telka!" on this mountain-side.
"Telka!" still I, pleading, cry;
Answer me the woods and sky,
And the lonely years go by.

On an evening dark and chill
Came a shadow up the hill,—
Came a spectre, grim and white
As a ghost that walks the night,
Grim and bowed, and with the cry
Of a wretch about to die,—
Came and fell and cried to me:
"It is Telka come!" said she.
So she fell and so she cried
On that lonely mountain-side
Where was Telka wont to bide.

"Who hath bribed those lips to lie?
Telka's face was fair," quoth I;
"Thine is furrowed with despair.
There is winter in thy hair;
But upon her beauteous head
Was there summer glory shed,—
Such a glory as the sun,
When his daily course is run,
Smiles upon this mountain height
As he kisses it good-night.
There was music in her tone,
Misery in thy voice alone.
They have bid thee lie to me.
Let me pass! Thou art not she!
Let my sorrow sacred be
Underneath this trysting tree!"

So in wrath I went my way,
And they came another day,—
Came another day, and said:
"Hush thy cry, for she is dead,
Yonder on the mountain-side
She is buried where she died,
Where you twain were wont to bide,
Where she came and fell and cried
Pardon that thy wrath denied;
And above her bosom grows
As in mockery the Rose:
It was white; but now 'tis red,
And in shame it bows its head
Over sinful Telka dead."

So they thought to silence me,—
As if love could silenced be!
Fool were I, and fools were they!
Scornfully I went my way,
And upon the mountain-side
"Telka!" evermore I cried.
"Telka!" evermore I cry;
Answer me the woods and sky:
So the lonely years go by.

She is lost, and that is all;
Sometime she shall hear my call,
Hear my pleading call, and then
Find her way to me again.

PLAINT OF THE MISSOURI 'COON IN THE BERLIN ZOÖLOGICAL GARDENS

Friend, by the way you hump yourself you're from the States, I know,
And born in old Mizzoorah, where the 'coons in plenty grow.
I, too, am native of that clime; but harsh, relentless fate
Has doomed me to an exile far from that noble State;
And I, who used to climb around, and swing from tree to tree,
Now lead a life of ignominious ease, as you can see.
Have pity, O compatriot mine! and bide a season near,
While I unfurl a dismal tale to catch your friendly ear.

My pedigree is noble: they used my grandsire's skin
To piece a coat for Patterson to warm himself within,—
Tom Patterson, of Denver; no ermine can compare
With the grizzled robe that Democratic statesman loves to wear.
Of such a grandsire I am come; and in the County Cole
All up an ancient cottonwood our family had its hole.
We envied not the liveried pomp nor proud estate of kings,

As we hustled round from day to day in search of bugs and things.

And when the darkness fell around, a mocking-bird was nigh,
Inviting pleasant, soothing dreams with his sweet lullaby;
And sometimes came the yellow dog to brag around all night
That nary 'coon could wallop him in a stand-up barrel fight.
We simply smiled and let him howl, for all Mizzoorians know
That ary 'coon can best a dog, if the coon gets half a show;
But we'd nestle close and shiver when the mellow moon had ris'n,
And the hungry nigger sought our lair in hopes to make us his'n.

Raised as I was, it's hardly strange I pine for those old days;
I cannot get acclimated, or used to German ways.
The victuals that they give me here may all be very fine
For vulgar, common palates, but they will not do for mine.
The 'coon that's been accustomed to stanch democratic cheer
Will not put up with onion tarts and sausage steeped in beer!
No; let the rest, for meat and drink, accede to slavish terms,
But send me back from whence I came, and let me grub for worms!

They come, these gaping Teutons do, on Sunday afternoons,
And wonder what I am,—alas, there are no German 'coons!
For if there were, I still might swing at home from tree to tree,
The symbol of democracy, that's woolly, blithe, and free.
And yet for what my captors are I would not change my lot,
For I have tasted liberty, these others they have not;
So, even caged, the democratic 'coon more glory feels
Than the conscript German puppets with their swords about their heels.

Well, give my love to Crittenden, to Clardy, and O'Neill,
To Jasper Burke and Col. Jones, and tell 'em how I feel;
My compliments to Cockrill, Stephens, Switzler, Francis, Vest,
Bill Nelson, J. West Goodwin, Jedge Broadhead, and the rest.
Bid them be steadfast in the faith, and pay no heed at all
To Joe McCullagh's badinage or Chauncey Filley's gall;
And urge them to retaliate for what I'm suffering here
By cinching all the alien class that wants its Sunday beer.

ARMENIAN LULLABY

If thou wilt close thy drowsy eyes,
My mulberry one, my golden son,
The rose shall sing thee lullabies,
My pretty cosset lambkin!
And thou shalt swing in an almond-tree,
With a flood of moonbeams rocking thee,—
A silver boat in a golden sea,—
My velvet love, my nestling dove,
My own pomegranate-blossom!

The stork shall guard thee passing well
All night, my sweet, my dimple-feet,
And bring thee myrrh and asphodel,
My gentle rain-of-springtime;
And for thy slumber-play shall twine
The diamond stars with an emerald vine,
To trail in the waves of ruby wine,
My hyacinth-bloom, my heart's perfume,
My cooing little turtle!

And when the morn wakes up to see
My apple-bright, my soul's delight,
The partridge shall come calling thee,
My jar of milk-and-honey!
Yes, thou shalt know what mystery lies
In the amethyst deep of the curtained skies,
If thou wilt fold thy onyx eyes,
You wakeful one, you naughty son,
You chirping little sparrow!

THE PARTRIDGE

As beats the sun from mountain crest,
With "Pretty, pretty,"
Cometh the partridge from her nest.
The flowers threw kisses sweet to her
(For all the flowers that bloomed knew her);
Yet hasteneth she to mine and me,—
Ah, pretty, pretty!
Ah, dear little partridge!

And when I hear the partridge cry
So pretty, pretty,
Upon the house-top breakfast I.
She comes a-chirping far and wide,
And swinging from the mountain-side
I see and hear the dainty dear,—
Ah, pretty, pretty!
Ah, dear little partridge!

Thy nest's inlaid with posies rare,
And pretty, pretty;
Bloom violet, rose, and lily there;
The place is full of balmy dew
(The tears of flowers in love with you!);
And one and all, impassioned, call,
"O pretty, pretty!
O dear little partridge!"

Thy feathers they are soft and sleek,—
So pretty, pretty!
Long is thy neck, and small thy beak,
The color of thy plumage far
More bright than rainbow colors are.
Sweeter than dove is she I love,—
My pretty, pretty!
My dear little partridge!

When comes the partridge from the tree,
So pretty, pretty,
And sings her little hymn to me,
Why, all the world is cheered thereby,
The heart leaps up into the eye,
And Echo then gives back again
Our "Pretty, pretty!"
Our "Dear little partridge!"

Admitting thee most blest of all,
And pretty, pretty,
The birds come with thee at thy call;
In flocks they come, and round thee play,
And this is what they seem to say,—
They say and sing, each feathered thing,
"Ah, pretty, pretty!
Ah, dear little partridge!"

CORINTHIAN HALL

Corinthian Hall is a tumble-down place,
Which some finical folks have pronounced a disgrace;
But once was a time when Corinthian Hall
Excited the rapture and plaudits of all,
With its carpeted stairs,
And its new yellow chairs,
And its stunning ensemble of citified airs.
Why, the Atchison Champion said 'twas the best
Of Thespian temples extant in the West.

It was new, and was ours,—that was ages ago,
Before opry had spoiled the legitimate show,—
It was new, and was ours! We could toss back the jeers
Our rivals had launched at our city for years.
Corinthian Hall!
Why, it discounted all
Other halls in the Valley, and well I recall
The night of the opening; from near and afar
Came the crowd to see Toodles performed by De Bar.

Oh, those days they were palmy, and never again
Shall earth see such genius as gladdened us then;
For actors were actors, and each one knew how
To whoop up his art in the sweat of his brow.
He'd a tragedy air, and wore copious hair;
And when he ate victuals, he ordered 'em rare.
Dame Fortune ne'er feazed him,—in fact, never could
When liquor was handy and walking was good.

And the shows in those days! Ah, how well I recall
The shows that I saw in Corinthian Hall!
Maggie Mitchell and Lotty were then in their prime;
And as for Jane Coombs, she was simply sublime;
And I'm ready to swear there is none could compare
With Breslau in Borgia, supported by Fair;
While in passionate rôles it was patent to us
That the great John A. Stevens was ne ultra plus.

And was there demand for the tribute of tears,
We had sweet Charlotte Thompson those halcyon years,
And wee Katie Putnam. The savants allow
That the like of Kate Fisher ain't visible now.
What artist to-day have we equal to Rae,
Or to sturdy Jack Langrishe? God rest 'em, I say!
And when died Buchanan, the "St. Joe Gazette"
Opined that the sun of our drama had set.

Corinthian Hall was devoted to song
When the Barnabee concert troupe happened along,
Or Ossian E. Dodge, or the Comical Brown,
Or the Holmans with William H. Crane struck our town;
But the one special card
That hit us all hard
Was Caroline Richings and Peter Bernard;
And the bells of the Bergers still ring in my ears;
And, oh, how I laughed at Sol Russell those years!

The Haverly Minstrels were boss in those days,
And our critics accorded them columns of praise;
They'd handsome mustaches and big cluster rings,
And their shirt fronts were blazing with diamonds and things;
They gave a parade, and sweet music they made
Every evening in front of the house where they played.
'Twixt posters and hand-bills the town was agog
For Primrose and West in their great statue clog.

Many years intervene, yet I'm free to maintain
That I doted on Chanfrau, McWade, and Frank Frayne;
Tom Stivers, the local, declared for a truth
That Mayo as Hamlet was better than Booth:

While in rôles that were thrillin', involving much killin',
Jim Wallick loomed up our ideal of a villain;
Mrs. Bowers, Alvin Joslin, Frank Aiken,—they all
Earned their titles to fame in Corinthian Hall.

But Time, as begrudging the glory that fell
On the spot I revere and remember so well,
Spent his spite on the timbers, the plaster, and paint,
And breathed on them all his morbiferous taint;
So the trappings of gold and the gear manifold
Got gangrened with rust and rheumatic with mould,
And we saw dank decay and oblivion fall,
Like vapors of night, on Corinthian Hall.

When the gas is ablaze in the opry at night,
And the music goes floating on billows of light,
Why, I often regret that I'm grown to a man,
And I pine to be back where my mission began,
And I'm fain to recall
Reminiscences all
That come with the thought of Corinthian Hall,—
To hear and to see what delighted me then,
And to revel in raptures of boyhood again.

Though Corinthian Hall is a tumble-down place,
Which some finical folks have pronounced a disgrace,
There is one young old boy, quite as worthy as they,
Who, aweary of art as expounded to-day,
Would surrender what gold
He's amassed to behold
A tithe of the wonderful doings of old,
A glimpse of the glories that used to enthrall
Our crême de la crême in Corinthian Hall.

THE RED, RED WEST

I've travelled in heaps of countries, and studied all kinds of art,
Till there isn't a critic or connoisseur who's properly deemed so smart;
And I'm free to say that the grand results of my explorations show
That somehow paint gets redder the farther out West I go.

I've sipped the voluptuous sherbet that the Orientals serve,
And I've felt the glow of red Bordeaux tingling each separate nerve;
I've sampled your classic Massic under an arbor green,
And I've reeked with song a whole night long over a brown poteen.

The stalwart brew of the land o' cakes, the schnapps of the frugal Dutch,
The much-praised wine of the distant Rhine, and the beer praised overmuch,
The ale of dear old London, and the port of Southern climes,—

All, ad infin., have I taken in a hundred thousand times.

Yet, as I afore-mentioned, these other charms are naught
Compared with the paramount gorgeousness with which the West is fraught;
For Art and Nature are just the same in the land where the porker grows,
And the paint keeps getting redder the farther out West one goes.

Our savants have never discovered the reason why this is so,
And ninety per cent of the laymen care less than the savants know;
It answers every purpose that this is manifest:
The paint keeps getting redder the farther you go out West.

Give me no home 'neath the pale pink dome of European skies,
No cot for me by the salmon sea that far to the southward lies;
But away out West I would build my nest on top of a carmine hill,
Where I can paint, without restraint, creation redder still!

THE THREE KINGS OF COLOGNE

From out Cologne there came three kings
To worship Jesus Christ, their King.
To Him they sought fine herbs they brought,
And many a beauteous golden thing;
They brought their gifts to Bethlehem town,
And in that manger set them down.

Then spake the first king, and he said:
"O Child, most heavenly, bright, and fair!
I bring this crown to Bethlehem town
For Thee, and only Thee, to wear;
So give a heavenly crown to me
When I shall come at last to Thee!"

The second, then. "I bring Thee here
This royal robe, O Child!" he cried;
"Of silk 'tis spun, and such an one
There is not in the world beside;
So in the day of doom requite
Me with a heavenly robe of white!"

The third king gave his gift, and quoth:
"Spikenard and myrrh to Thee I bring,
And with these twain would I most fain
Anoint the body of my King;
So may their incense sometime rise
To plead for me in yonder skies!"

Thus spake the three kings of Cologne,
That gave their gifts, and went their way;

And now kneel I in prayer hard by
The cradle of the Child to-day;
Nor crown, nor robe, nor spice I bring
As offering unto Christ, my King.

Yet have I brought a gift the Child
May not despise, however small;
For here I lay my heart to-day,
And it is full of love to all.
Take Thou the poor but loyal thing,
My only tribute, Christ, my King!

IPSWICH

In Ipswich nights are cool and fair,
And the voice that comes from the yonder sea
Sings to the quaint old mansions there
Of "the time, the time that used to be;"
And the quaint old mansions rock and groan,
And they seem to say in an undertone,
With half a sigh and with half a moan:
"It was, but it never again will be."

In Ipswich witches weave at night
Their magic, spells with impish glee;
They shriek and laugh in their demon flight
From the old Main House to the frightened sea.
And ghosts of eld come out to weep
Over the town that is fast asleep;
And they sob and they wail, as on they creep:
"It was, but it never again will be."

In Ipswich riseth Heart-Break Hill
Over against the calling sea;
And through the nights so deep and chill
Watcheth a maiden constantly,—
Watcheth alone, nor seems to hear
Over the roar of the waves anear
The pitiful cry of a far-off year:
"It was, but it never again will be."

In Ipswich once a witch I knew,—
An artless Saxon witch was she;
By that flaxen hair and those eyes of blue,
Sweet was the spell she cast on me.
Alas! but the years have wrought me ill,
And the heart that is old and battered and chill
Seeketh again on Heart-Break Hill
What was, but never again can be.

Dear Anna, I would not conjure down
The ghost that cometh to solace me;
I love to think of old Ipswich town,
Where somewhat better than friends were we;
For with every thought of the dear old place
Cometh again the tender grace
Of a Saxon witch's pretty face,
As it was, and is, and ever shall be.

BILL'S TENOR AND MY BASS

Bill was short and dapper, while I was thin and tall;
I had flowin' whiskers, but Bill had none at all;
Clothes would never seem to set so nice on me as him,—
Folks used to laugh, and say I was too powerful slim,—
But Bill's clothes fit him like the paper on the wall;
And we were the sparkin'est beaus in all the place
When Bill sung tenor and I sung bass.

Cyrus Baker's oldest girl was member of the choir,—
Eyes as black as Kelsey's cat, and cheeks as red as fire!
She had the best sopranner voice I think I ever heard,—
Sung "Coronation," "Burlington," and "Chiny" like a bird;
Never done better than with Bill a-standin' nigh 'er,
A-holdin' of her hymn-book so she wouldn't lose the place,
When Bill sung tenor and I sung bass.

Then there was Prudence Hubbard, so cosey-like and fat,—
She sung alto, and wore a pee-wee hat;
Beaued her around one winter, and, first thing I knew,
One evenin' on the portico I up and called her "Prue"!
But, sakes alive! she didn't mind a little thing like that;
On all the works of Providence she set a cheerful face
When Bill was singin' tenor and I was singin' bass.

Bill, nevermore we two shall share the fun we used to then,
Nor know the comfort and the peace we had together when
We lived in Massachusetts in the good old courtin' days,
And lifted up our voices in psalms and hymns of praise.
Oh, how I wisht that I could live them happy times again!
For life, as we boys knew it, had a sweet, peculiar grace
When you was singin' tenor and I was singin' bass.

The music folks have nowadays ain't what it used to be,
Because there ain't no singers now on earth like Bill and me.
Why, Lemuel Bangs, who used to go to Springfield twice a year,
Admitted that for singin' Bill and me had not a peer
When Bill went soarin' up to A and I dropped down to D!

The old bull-fiddle Beza Dimmitt played warn't in the race
'Longside of Bill's high tenor and my sonorious bass.

Bill moved to Californy in the spring of '54,
And we folks that used to know him never knew him any more;
Then Cyrus Baker's oldest girl, she kind o' pined a spell,
And, hankerin' after sympathy, it naterally befell
That she married Deacon Pitkin's boy, who kep' the general store;
And so the years, the changeful years, have rattled on apace
Since Bill sung tenor and I sung bass.

As I was settin' by the stove this evenin' after tea,
I noticed wife kep' hitchin' close and closer up to me;
And as she patched the gingham frock our gran'child wore to-day,
I heerd her gin a sigh that seemed to come from fur away.
Couldn't help inquirin' what the trouble might be;
"Was thinkin' of the time," says Prue, a-breshin' at her face,
"When Bill sung tenor and you sung bass."

FIDUCIT

Three comrades on the German Rhine,
Defying care and weather,
Together quaffed the mellow wine,
And sung their songs together.
What recked they of the griefs of life,
With wine and song to cheer them?
Though elsewhere trouble might be rife,
It would not come anear them.

Anon one comrade passed away,
And presently another,
And yet unto the tryst each day
Repaired the lonely brother;
And still, as gayly as of old,
That third one, hero-hearted,
Filled to the brim each cup of gold,
And called to the departed,—

"O comrades mine! I see ye not,
Nor hear your kindly greeting,
Yet in this old, familiar spot
Be still our loving meeting!
Here have I filled each bouting-cup
With juices red and cheery;
I pray ye drink the portion up,
And as of old make merry!"

And once before his tear-dimmed eyes,

All in the haunted gloaming,
He saw two ghostly figures rise,
And quaff the beakers foaming;
He heard two spirit voices call,
"Fiducit, jovial brother!"
And so forever from that hall
Went they with one another.

THE "ST. JO GAZETTE"

When I helped 'em run the local on the "St. Jo Gazette,"
I was upon familiar terms with every one I met;
For "items" were my stock in trade in that my callow time,
Before the muses tempted me to try my hand at rhyme,—
Before I found in verses
Those soothing, gracious mercies,
Less practical, but much more glorious than a well-filled purse is.
A votary of Mammon, I hustled round and sweat,
And helped 'em run the local on the "St. Jo Gazette."

The labors of the day began at half-past eight A.M.,
For the farmers came in early, and I had to tackle them;
And many a noble bit of news I managed to acquire
By those discreet attentions which all farmer-folk admire,
With my daily commentary
On affairs of farm and dairy,
The tone of which anon with subtle pufferies I'd vary,—
Oh, many a peck of apples and of peaches did I get
When I helped 'em run the local on the "St. Jo Gazette."

Dramatic news was scarce, but when a minstrel show was due,
Why, Milton Tootle's opera house was then my rendezvous;
Judge Grubb would give me points about the latest legal case,
And Dr. Runcie let me print his sermons when I'd space;
Of fevers, fractures, humors,
Contusions, fits, and tumors,
Would Dr. Hall or Dr. Baines confirm or nail the rumors;
From Colonel Dawes what railroad news there was I used to get,—
When I helped 'em run the local on the "St. Jo Gazette."

For "personals" the old Pacific House was just the place,—
Pap Abell knew the pedigrees of all the human race;
And when he'd gin up all he had, he'd drop a subtle wink,
And lead the way where one might wet one's whistle with a drink.
Those drinks at the Pacific,
When days were sudorific,
Were what Parisians (pray excuse my French!) would call "magnifique;"
And frequently an invitation to a meal I'd get
When I helped 'em run the local on the "St. Jo Gazette."

And when in rainy weather news was scarce as well as slow,
To Saxton's bank or Hopkins' store for items would I go.
The jokes which Colonel Saxton told were old, but good enough
For local application in lieu of better stuff;
And when the ducks were flying,
Or the fishing well worth trying—
Gosh! but those "sports" at Hopkins' store could beat the world at lying!
And I—I printed all their yarns, though not without regret,
When I helped 'em run the local on the "St. Jo Gazette."

For squibs political I'd go to Col. Waller Young,
Or Col. James N. Burnes, the "statesman with the silver tongue;"
Should some old pioneer take sick and die, why, then I'd call
On Frank M. Posegate for the "life," and Posegate knew 'em all.
Lon Tullar used to pony
Up descriptions that were tony
Of toilets worn at party, ball, or conversazione;
For the ladies were addicted to the style called "deckolett"
When I helped 'em run the local on the "St. Jo Gazette."

So was I wont my daily round of labor to pursue;
And when came night I found that there was still more work to do,—
The telegraph to edit, yards and yards of proof to read,
And reprint to be gathered to supply the printers' greed.
Oh, but it takes agility,
Combined with versatility,
To run a country daily with appropriate ability!
There never were a smarter lot of editors, I'll bet,
Than we who whooped up local on the "St. Jo Gazette."

Yes, maybe it was irksome; maybe a discontent
Rebellious rose amid the toil I daily underwent
If so, I don't remember; this only do I know,—
My thoughts turn ever fondly to that time in old St. Jo.
The years that speed so fleetly
Have blotted out completely
All else than that which still remains to solace me so sweetly;
The friendships of that time,—ah, me! they are as precious yet
As when I was a local on the "St. Jo Gazette."

IN AMSTERDAM

Meynheer Hans Von Der Bloom has got
A majazin in Kalverstraat,
Where one may buy for sordid gold
Wares quaint and curious, new and old.
Here are antiquities galore,—
The jewels which Dutch monarchs wore,
Swords, teacups, helmets, platters, clocks,

Bright Dresden jars, dull Holland crocks,
And all those joys I might rehearse
That please the eye, but wreck the purse.

I most admired an ancient bed,
With ornate carvings at its head,—
A massive frame of dingy oak,
Whose curious size and mould bespoke
Prodigious age. "How much?" I cried.
"Ein tousand gildens," Hans replied;
And then the honest Dutchman said
A king once owned that glorious bed,—
King Fritz der Foorst, of blessed fame,
Had owned and slept within the same!

Then long I stood and mutely gazed,
By reminiscent splendors dazed,
And I had bought it right away,
Had I the wherewithal to pay.
But, lacking of the needed pelf,
I thus discoursed within myself:
"O happy Holland! where's the bliss
That can approximate to this
Possession of the rare antique
Which maniacs hanker for and seek?
My native land is full of stuff
That's good, but is not old enough.
Alas! it has no oaken beds
Wherein have slumbered royal heads,
No relic on whose face we see
The proof of grand antiquity."

Thus reasoned I a goodly spell
Until, perchance, my vision fell
Upon a trademark at the head
Of Fritz der Foorst's old oaken bed,—
A rampant wolverine, and round
This strange device these words I found:
"Patent Antique. Birkey & Gay,
Grand Rapids, Michigan, U. S. A."

At present I'm not saying much
About the simple, guileless Dutch;
And as it were a loathsome spot
I keep away from Kalverstraat,
Determined when I want a bed
In which hath slept a royal head
I'll patronize no middleman,
But deal direct with Michigan.

TO THE PASSING SAINT

As to-night you came your way,
Bearing earthward heavenly joy,
Tell me, O dear saint, I pray,
Did you see my little boy?

By some fairer voice beguiled,
Once he wandered from my sight;
He is such a little child,
He should have my love this night.

It has been so many a year,—
Oh, so many a year since then!
Yet he was so very dear,
Surely he will come again.

If upon your way you see
One whose beauty is divine,
Will you send him back to me?
He is lost, and he is mine.

Tell him that his little chair
Nestles where the sunbeams meet,
That the shoes he used to wear
Yearn to kiss his dimpled feet.

Tell him of each pretty toy
That was wont to share his glee;
Maybe that will bring my boy
Back to them and back to me.

O dear saint, as on you go
Through the glad and sparkling frost,
Bid those bells ring high and low
For a little child that's lost!

O dear saint, that blessest men
With the grace of Christmas joy,
Soothe this heart with love again,—
Give me back my little boy!

THE FISHERMAN'S FEAST

Of all the gracious gifts of Spring,
Is there another can surpass
This delicate, voluptuous thing,—
This dapple-green, plump-shouldered bass?

Upon a damask napkin laid,
What exhalations superfine
Our gustatory nerves pervade,
Provoking quenchless thirsts for wine!

The ancients loved this noble fish;
And, coming from the kitchen fire
All piping hot upon a dish,
What raptures did he not inspire?
"Fish should swim twice," they used to say,—
Once in their native, vapid brine,
And then again, a better way—
You understand; fetch on the wine!

Ah, dainty monarch of the flood,
How often have I cast for you,
How often sadly seen you scud
Where weeds and water-lilies grew!
How often have you filched my bait,
How often snapped my treacherous line!
Yet here I have you on this plate,—
You shall swim twice, and now in wine.

And, harkee, garçon! let the blood
Of cobwebbed years be spilled for him,—
Ay, in a rich Burgundian flood
This piscatorial pride should swim;
So, were he living, he would say
He gladly died for me and mine,
And, as it were his native spray,
He'd lash the sauce—what, ho! the wine!

I would it were ordained for me
To share your fate, O finny friend!
I surely were not loath to be
Reserved for such a noble end;
For when old Chronos, gaunt and grim,
At last reels in his ruthless line,
What were my ecstasy to swim
In wine, in wine, in glorious wine!

Well, here's a health to you, sweet Spring!
And, prithee, whilst I stick to earth,
Come hither every year and bring
The boons provocative of mirth;
And should your stock of bass run low,
However much I might repine,
I think I might survive the blow,
If plied with wine and still more wine!

NIGHTFALL IN DORDRECHT

The mill goes toiling slowly around
With steady and solemn creak,
And my little one hears in the kindly sound
The voice of the old mill speak;
While round and round those big white wings
Grimly and ghostlike creep,
My little one hears that the old mill sings,
"Sleep, little tulip, sleep!"

The sails are reefed and the nets are drawn,
And over his pot of beer
The fisher, against the morrow's dawn,
Lustily maketh cheer;
He mocks at the winds that caper along
From the far-off, clamorous deep,
But we—we love their lullaby-song
Of "Sleep, little tulip, sleep!"

Old dog Fritz, in slumber sound,
Groans of the stony mart;
To-morrow how proudly he'll trot you around,
Hitched to our new milk-cart!
And you shall help me blanket the kine,
And fold the gentle sheep,
And set the herring a-soak in brine,—
But now, little tulip, sleep!

A Dream-One comes to button the eyes
That wearily droop and blink,
While the old mill buffets the frowning skies,
And scolds at the stars that wink;
Over your face the misty wings
Of that beautiful Dream-One sweep,
And, rocking your cradle, she softly sings,
"Sleep, little tulip, sleep!"

THE ONION TART

Of tarts there be a thousand kinds,
So versatile the art,
And, as we all have different minds,
Each has his favorite tart;
But those which most delight the rest
Methinks should suit me not:
The onion tart doth please me best,—
Ach, Gott! mein lieber Gott!

Where but in Deutschland can be found
This boon of which I sing?
Who but a Teuton could compound
This sui generis thing?
None with the German frau can vie
In arts cuisine, I wot,
Whose summum bonum breeds the sigh,
"Ach, Gott! mein lieber Gott!"

You slice the fruit upon the dough,
And season to the taste,
Then in an oven (not too slow)
The viand should be placed;
And when 'tis done, upon a plate
You serve it piping hot.
Your nostrils and your eyes dilate,—
Ach, Gott! mein lieber Gott!

It sweeps upon the sight and smell
In overwhelming tide,
And then the sense of taste as well
Betimes is gratified:
Three noble senses drowned in bliss!
I prithee tell me, what
Is there beside compares with this?
Ach, Gott! mein lieber Gott!

For if the fruit be proper young,
And if the crust be good,
How shall they melt upon the tongue
Into a savory flood!
How seek the Mecca down below,
And linger round that spot,
Entailing weeks and months of woe,—
Ach, Gott! mein lieber Gott!

If Nature gives men appetites
For things that won't digest,
Why, let them eat whatso delights,
And let her stand the rest;
And though the sin involve the cost
Of Carlsbad, like as not
'Tis better to have loved and lost,—
Ach, Gott! mein lieber Gott!

Beyond the vast, the billowy tide,
Where my compatriots dwell,
All kinds of victuals have I tried,
All kinds of drinks, as well;
But nothing known to Yankee art

Appears to reach the spot
Like this Teutonic onion tart,—
Ach, Gott! mein lieber Gott!

So, though I quaff of Carlsbad's tide
As full as I can hold,
And for complete reform inside
Plank down my horde of gold,
Remorse shall not consume my heart,
Nor sorrow vex my lot,
For I have eaten onion tart,—
Ach, Gott! mein lieber Gott!

GRANDMA'S BOMBAZINE

It's everywhere that women fair invite and please my eye,
And that on dress I lay much stress I can't and sha'n't deny:
The English dame who's all aflame with divers colors bright,
The Teuton belle, the ma'moiselle,—all give me keen delight;
And yet I'll say, go where I may, I never yet have seen
A dress that's quite as grand a sight as was that bombazine.

Now, you must know 'twas years ago this quaint but noble gown
Flashed in one day, the usual way, upon our solemn town.
'Twas Fisk who sold for sordid gold that gravely scrumptious thing,—
Jim Fisk, the man who drove a span that would have joyed a king,—
And grandma's eye fell with a sigh upon that sombre sheen,
And grandpa's purse looked much the worse for grandma's bombazine.

Though ten years old, I never told the neighbors of the gown;
For grandma said, "This secret, Ned, must not be breathed in town."
The sitting-room for days of gloom was in a dreadful mess
When that quaint dame, Miss Kelsey, came to make the wondrous dress:
To fit and baste and stitch a waist, with whale-bones in between,
Is precious slow, as all folks know who've made a bombazine.

With fortitude dear grandma stood the trial to the end
(The nerve we find in womankind I cannot comprehend!);
And when 'twas done resolved that none should guess at the surprise,
Within the press she hid that dress, secure from prying eyes;
For grandma knew a thing or two,—by which remark I mean
That Sundays were the days for her to wear that bombazine.

I need not state she got there late; and, sailing up the aisle
With regal grace, on grandma's face reposed a conscious smile.
It fitted so, above, below, and hung so well all round,
That there was not one faulty spot a critic could have found.
How proud I was of her, because she looked so like a queen!
And that was why, perhaps, that I admired the bombazine.

But there were those, as you'd suppose, who scorned that perfect gown;
For ugly-grained old cats obtained in that New England town:
The Widow White spat out her spite in one: "It doesn't fit!"
The Packard girls (they wore false curls) all giggled like to split;
Sophronia Wade, the sour old maid, she turned a bilious green,
When she descried that joy and pride, my grandma's bombazine.

But grandma knew, and I did, too, that gown was wondrous fine,—
The envious sneers and jaundiced jeers were a conclusive sign.
Why, grandpa said it went ahead of all the girls in town,
And, saying this, he snatched a kiss that like to burst that gown;
But, blushing red, my grandma said, "Oh, isn't grandpa mean!"
Yet evermore my grandma wore his favorite bombazine.

And when she died that sombre pride passed down to heedless heirs,—
Alas, the day 't was hung away beneath the kitchen stairs!
Thence in due time, with dust and grime, came foes on foot and wing,
And made their nests and sped their guests in that once beauteous thing.
'Tis so, forsooth! Time's envious tooth corrodes each human scene;
And so, at last, to ruin passed my grandma's bombazine.

Yet to this day, I'm proud to say, it plays a grateful part,—
The thoughts it brings are of such things as touch and warm my heart.
This gown, my dear, you show me here I'll own is passing fair,
Though I'll confess it's no such dress as grandma used to wear.
Yet wear it, do; perchance when you and I are off the scene,
Our boy shall sing this comely thing as I the bombazine.

RARE ROAST BEEF

When the numerous distempers to which all flesh is heir
Torment us till our very souls are reeking with despair;
When that monster fiend, Dyspepsy, rears its spectral hydra head,
Filling bon vivants and epicures with certain nameless dread;
When any ill of body or of intellect abounds,
Be it sickness known to Galen or disease unknown to Lowndes,—
In such a dire emergency it is my firm belief
That there is no diet quite so good as rare roast beef.

And even when the body's in the very prime of health,
When sweet contentment spreads upon the cheeks her rosy wealth,
And when a man devours three meals per day and pines for more,
And growls because instead of three square meals there are not four,—
Well, even then, though cake and pie do service on the side,
And coffee is a luxury that may not be denied,
Still of the many viands there is one that's hailed as chief,
And that, as you are well aware, is rare roast beef.

Some like the sirloin, but I think the porterhouse is best,—
'Tis juicier and tenderer and meatier than the rest;
Put on this roast a dash of salt, and then of water pour
Into the sizzling dripping-pan a cupful, and no more;
The oven being hot, the roast will cook in half an hour;
Then to the juices in the pan you add a little flour,
And so you get a gravy that is called the cap sheaf
Of that glorious summum bonum, rare roast beef.

Served on a platter that is hot, and carved with thin, keen knife,
How does this savory viand enhance the worth of life!
Give me no thin and shadowy slice, but a thick and steaming slab,—
Who would not choose a generous hunk to a bloodless little dab?
Upon a nice hot plate how does the juicy morceau steam,
A symphony in scarlet or a red incarnate dream!
Take from me eyes and ears and all, O Time, thou ruthless thief!
Except these teeth wherewith to deal with rare roast beef.

Most every kind and rôle of modern victuals have I tried,
Including roasted, fricasseed, broiled, toasted, stewed, and fried,
Your canvasbacks and papa-bottes and muttonchops subese,
Your patties à la Turkey and your doughnuts à la grease;
I've whirled away dyspeptic hours with crabs in marble halls,
And in the lowly cottage I've experienced codfish balls;
But I've never found a viand that could so allay all grief
And soothe the cockles of the heart as rare roast beef.

I honor that sagacious king who, in a grateful mood,
Knighted the savory loin that on the royal table stood;
And as for me I'd ask no better friend than this good roast,
Which is my squeamish stomach's fortress (feste Burg) and host;
For with this ally with me I can mock Dyspepsy's wrath,
Can I pursue the joy of Wisdom's pleasant, peaceful path.
So I do off my vest and let my waistband out a reef
When I soever set me down to rare roast beef.

GANDERFEATHER'S GIFT

I was just a little thing
When a fairy came and kissed me;
Floating in upon the light
Of a haunted summer night,
Lo! the fairies came to sing
Pretty slumber songs, and bring
Certain boons that else had missed me.
From a dream I turned to see
What those strangers brought for me,
When that fairy up and kissed me,—
Here, upon this cheek, he kissed me!

Simmerdew was there, but she
Did not like me altogether;
Daisybright and Turtledove,
Pilfercurds and Honeylove,
Thistleblow and Amberglee
On that gleaming, ghostly sea
Floated from the misty heather,
And around my trundle-bed
Frisked and looked and whispering said,
Solemn-like and all together:
"You shall kiss him, Ganderfeather!"

Ganderfeather kissed me then,—
Ganderfeather, quaint and merry!
No attenuate sprite was he,
But as buxom as could be;
Kissed me twice and once again,
And the others shouted when
On my cheek uprose a berry
Somewhat like a mole, mayhap,
But the kiss-mark of that chap
Ganderfeather, passing merry,—
Humorsome but kindly, very!

I was just a tiny thing
When the prankish Ganderfeather
Brought this curious gift to me
With his fairy kisses three;
Yet with honest pride I sing
That same gift he chose to bring
Out of yonder haunted heather;
Other charms and friendships fly,—
Constant friends this mole and I,
Who have been so long together!
Thank you, little Ganderfeather!

OLD TIMES, OLD FRIENDS, OLD LOVE

There are no days like the good old days,—
The days when we were youthful!
When humankind were pure of mind,
And speech and deeds were truthful;
Before a love for sordid gold
Became man's ruling passion,
And before each dame and maid became
Slave to the tyrant fashion!

There are no girls like the good old girls,—

Against the world I'd stake 'em!
As buxom and smart and clean of heart
As the Lord knew how to make 'em!
They were rich in spirit and common-sense,
And piety all supportin';
They could bake and brew, and had taught school, too,
And they made such likely courtin'!

There are no boys like the good old boys,—
When we were boys together!
When the grass was sweet to the brown bare feet
That dimpled the laughing heather;
When the pewee sung to the summer dawn
Of the bee in the billowy clover,
Or down by the mill the whip-poor-will
Echoed his night song over.

There is no love like the good old love,—
The love that mother gave us!
We are old, old men, yet we pine again
For that precious grace,—God save us!
So we dream and dream of the good old times,
And our hearts grow tenderer, fonder,
As those dear old dreams bring soothing gleams
Of heaven away off yonder.

OUR WHIPPINGS

Come, Harvey, let us sit awhile and talk about the times
Before you went to selling clothes and I to peddling rhymes,—
The days when we were little boys, as naughty little boys
As ever worried home folks with their everlasting noise!
Egad! and were we so disposed, I'll venture we could show
The scars of wallopings we got some forty years ago;
What wallopings I mean I think I need not specify,—
Mother's whippings didn't hurt; but father's,—oh, my!

The way that we played hookey those many years ago,
We'd rather give 'most anything than have our children know!
The thousand naughty things we did, the thousand fibs we told,—
Why, thinking of them makes my Presbyterian blood run cold!
How often Deacon Sabine Morse remarked if we were his
He'd tan our "pesky little hides until the blisters riz"!
It's many a hearty thrashing to that Deacon Morse we owe,—
Mother's whippings didn't count; father's did, though!

We used to sneak off swimmin' in those careless, boyish days,
And come back home of evenings with our necks and backs ablaze;
How mother used to wonder why our clothes were full of sand,—

But father, having been a boy, appeared to understand;
And after tea he'd beckon us to join him in the shed,
Where he'd proceed to tinge our backs a deeper, darker red.
Say what we will of mother's, there is none will controvert
The proposition that our father's lickings always hurt!

For mother was by nature so forgiving and so mild
That she inclined to spare the rod although she spoiled the child;
And when at last in self-defence she had to whip us, she
Appeared to feel those whippings a great deal more than we:
But how we bellowed and took on, as if we'd like to die,—
Poor mother really thought she hurt, and that's what made her cry!
Then how we youngsters snickered as out the door we slid,
For mother's whippings never hurt, though father's always did!

In after years poor father simmered down to five feet four,
But in our youth he seemed to us in height eight feet or more!
Oh, how we shivered when he quoth in cold, suggestive tone:
"I'll see you in the woodshed after supper all alone!"
Oh, how the legs and arms and dust and trouser-buttons flew,—
What florid vocalisms marked that vesper interview!
Yes, after all this lapse of years, I feelingly assert,
With all respect to mother, it was father's whippings hurt!

The little boy experiencing that tingling 'neath his vest
Is often loath to realize that all is for the best;
Yet, when the boy gets older, he pictures with delight
The bufferings of childhood,—as we do here to-night.
The years, the gracious years, have smoothed and beautified the ways
That to our little feet seemed all too rugged in the days
Before you went to selling clothes and I to peddling rhymes,—
So, Harvey, let us sit awhile and think upon those times.

BION'S SONG OF EROS

Eros is the god of love;
He and I are hand-in-glove.
All the gentle, gracious Muses
Follow Eros where he leads,
And they bless the bard who chooses
To proclaim love's famous deeds;
Him they serve in rapturous glee,—
That is why they're good to me.

Sometimes I have gone astray
From love's sunny, flowery way:
How I floundered, how I stuttered!
And, deprived of ways and means,
What egregious rot I uttered,—

Such as suits the magazines!
I was rescued only when
Eros called me back again.

Gods forefend that I should shun
That benignant Mother's son!
Why, the poet who refuses
To emblazon love's delights
Gets the mitten from the Muses,—
Then what balderdash he writes!
I love Love; which being so,
See how smooth my verses flow!

Gentle Eros, lead the way,—
I will follow while I may:
Be thy path by hill or hollow,
I will follow fast and free;
And when I'm too old to follow,
I will sit and sing of thee,—
Potent still in intellect,
Sit, and sing, and retrospect.

MR. BILLINGS OF LOUISVILLE

There are times in one's life which one cannot forget;
And the time I remember's the evening I met
A haughty young scion of bluegrass renown
Who made my acquaintance while painting the town:
A handshake, a cocktail, a smoker, and then
Mr. Billings of Louisville touched me for ten.

There flowed in his veins the blue blood of the South,
And a cynical smile curled his sensuous mouth;
He quoted from Lanier and Poe by the yard,
But his purse had been hit by the war, and hit hard:
I felt that he honored and flattered me when
Mr. Billings of Louisville touched me for ten.

I wonder that never again since that night
A vision of Billings has hallowed my sight;
I pine for the sound of his voice and the thrill
That comes with the touch of a ten-dollar bill:
I wonder and pine; for—I say it again—
Mr. Billings of Louisville touched me for ten.

I've heard what old Whittier sung of Miss Maud;
But all such philosophy's nothing but fraud;
To one who's a bear in Chicago to-day,
With wheat going up, and the devil to pay,

These words are the saddest of tongue or of pen:
"Mr. Billings of Louisville touched me for ten."

POET AND KING

Though I am king, I have no throne
Save this rough wooden siege alone;
I have no empire, yet my sway
Extends a myriad leagues away;
No servile vassal bends his knee
In grovelling reverence to me,
Yet at my word all hearts beat high,
And there is fire in every eye,
And love and gratitude they bring
As tribute unto me, a king.

The folk that throng the busy street
Know not it is a king they meet;
And I am glad there is not seen
The monarch in my face and mien.
I should not choose to be the cause
Of fawning or of coarse applause:
I am content to know the arts
Wherewith to lord it o'er their hearts;
For when unto their hearts I sing,
I am a king, I am a king!

My sceptre,—see, it is a pen!
Wherewith I rule these hearts of men.
Sometime it pleaseth to beguile
Its monarch fancy with a smile;
Sometime it is athirst for tears:
And so adown the laurelled years
I walk, the noblest lord on earth,
Dispensing sympathy and mirth.
Aha! it is a magic thing
That makes me what I am,—a king!

Let empires crumble as they may,
Proudly I hold imperial sway;
The sunshine and the rain of years
Are human smiles and human tears
That come or vanish at my call,—
I am the monarch of them all!
Mindful alone of this am I:
The songs I sing shall never die;
Not even envious Death can wring
His glory from so great a king.

Come, brother, be a king with me,
And rule mankind eternally;
Lift up the weak, and cheer the strong,
Defend the truth, combat the wrong!
You'll find no sceptre like the pen
To hold and sway the hearts of men;
Its edicts flow in blood and tears
That will outwash the flood of years:
So, brother, sing your songs, oh, sing!
And be with me a king, a king!

LYDIA DICK

When I was a boy at college,
Filling up with classic knowledge,
Frequently I wondered why
Old Professor Demas Bentley
Used to praise so eloquently
"Opera Horatii."

Toiling on a season longer
Till my reasoning powers got stronger,
As my observation grew,
I became convinced that mellow,
Massic-loving poet fellow,
Horace, knew a thing or two.

Yes, we sophomores figured duly
That, if we appraised him truly,
Horace must have been a brick;
And no wonder that with ranting
Rhymes he went a-gallivanting
Round with sprightly Lydia Dick!

For that pink of female gender
Tall and shapely was, and slender,
Plump of neck and bust and arms;
While the raiment that invested
Her so jealously suggested
Certain more potential charms.

Those dark eyes of hers that fired him,
Those sweet accents that inspired him,
And her crown of glorious hair,—
These things baffle my description:
I should have a fit conniption
If I tried; so I forbear.

Maybe Lydia had her betters;

Anyway, this man of letters
Took that charmer as his pick.
Glad—yes, glad I am to know it!
I, a fin de siècle poet,
Sympathize with Lydia Dick!

Often in my arbor shady
I fall thinking of that lady,
And the pranks she used to play;
And I'm cheered,—for all we sages
Joy when from those distant ages
Lydia dances down our way.

Otherwise some folks might wonder,
With good reason, why in thunder
Learned professors, dry and prim,
Find such solace in the giddy
Pranks that Horace played with Liddy
Or that Liddy played on him.

Still this world of ours rejoices
In those ancient singing voices,
And our hearts beat high and quick,
To the cadence of old Tiber
Murmuring praise of roistering Liber
And of charming Lydia Dick.

Still Digentia, downward flowing,
Prattleth to the roses blowing
By the dark, deserted grot.
Still Soracte, looming lonely,
Watcheth for the coming only
Of a ghost that cometh not.

LIZZIE

I wonder ef all wimmin air
Like Lizzie is when we go out
To theaters an' concerts where
Is things the papers talk about.
Do other wimmin fret an' stew
Like they wuz bein' crucified,—
Frettin' a show or concert through,
With wonderin' ef the baby cried?

Now Lizzie knows that gran'ma's there
To see that everything is right;
Yet Lizzie thinks that gran'ma's care
Ain't good enuff f'r baby, quite.

Yet what am I to answer when
She kind uv fidgets at my side,
An' asks me every now an' then,
"I wonder ef the baby cried"?

Seems like she seen two little eyes
A-pinin' f'r their mother's smile;
Seems like she heern the pleadin' cries
Uv one she thinks uv all the while;
An' so she's sorry that she come.
An' though she allus tries to hide
The truth, she'd ruther stay to hum
Than wonder ef the baby cried.

Yes, wimmin folks is all alike—
By Lizzie you kin jedge the rest;
There never wuz a little tyke,
But that his mother loved him best.
And nex' to bein' what I be—
The husband uv my gentle bride—
I'd wisht I wuz that croodlin' wee,
With Lizzie wonderin' ef I cried.

LITTLE HOMER'S SLATE

After dear old grandma died,
Hunting through an oaken chest
In the attic, we espied
What repaid our childish quest:
'Twas a homely little slate,
Seemingly of ancient date.

On its quaint and battered face
Was the picture of a cart
Drawn with all that awkward grace
Which betokens childish art.
But what meant this legend, pray:
"Homer drew this yesterday"?

Mother recollected then
What the years were fain to hide:
She was but a baby when
Little Homer lived and died.
Forty years, so mother said,
Little Homer had been dead.

This one secret through those years
Grandma kept from all apart,
Hallowed by her lonely tears

And the breaking of her heart;
While each year that sped away
Seemed to her but yesterday.

So the homely little slate
Grandma's baby's fingers pressed,
To a memory consecrate,
Lieth in the oaken chest,
Where, unwilling we should know,
Grandma put it years ago.

ALWAYS RIGHT

Don't take on so, Hiram,
But do what you're told to do;
It's fair to suppose that yer mother knows
A heap sight more than you.
I'll allow that sometimes her way
Don't seem the wisest, quite;
But the easiest way,
When she's had her say,
Is to reckon yer mother is right.

Courted her ten long winters,
Saw her to singin'-school;
When she went down one spell to town,
I cried like a durned ol' fool;
Got mad at the boys for callin'
When I sparked her Sunday night:
But she said she knew
A thing or two,—
An' I reckoned yer mother wuz right.

I courted till I wuz aging,
And she wuz past her prime,—
I'd have died, I guess, if she hadn't said yes
When I popped f'r the hundredth time.
Said she'd never have took me
If I hadn't stuck so tight;
Opined that we
Could never agree,—
And I reckon yer mother wuz right!

"TROT, MY GOOD STEED, TROT!"

Where my true love abideth
I make my way to-night;

Lo! waiting, she
Espieth me,
And calleth in delight:
"I see his steed anear
Come trotting with my dear,—
Oh, idle not, good steed, but trot,
Trot thou my lover here!"

Aloose I cast the bridle,
And ply the whip and spur;
And gayly I
Speed this reply,
While faring on to her:
"Oh, true love, fear thou not!
I seek our trysting spot;
And double feed be yours, my steed,
If you more swiftly trot."

I vault from out the saddle,
And make my good steed fast;
Then to my breast
My love is pressed,—
At last, true heart, at last!
The garden drowsing lies,
The stars fold down their eyes,—
In this dear spot, my steed, neigh not,
Nor stamp in restless wise!

O passing sweet communion
Of young hearts, warm and true!
To thee belongs
The old, old songs
Love finds forever new.
We sing those songs, and then
Cometh the moment when
It's, "Good steed, trot from this dear spot,—
Trot, trot me home again!"

PROVIDENCE AND THE DOG

When I was young and callow, which was many years ago,
Within me the afflatus went surging to and fro;
And so I wrote a tragedy that fairly reeked with gore,
With every act concluding with the dead piled on the floor,—
A mighty effort, by the gods! and after I had read
The manuscript to Daly, that dramatic censor said:
"The plot is most exciting, and I like the dialogue;
You should take the thing to Providence, and try it on a dog."

McCambridge organized a troupe, including many a name
Unknown alike to guileless me, to riches, and to fame.
A pompous man whose name was Rae was Nestor of this troupe,—
Amphibious, he was quite at home outside or in the soup!
The way McCambridge billed him! Why, such dreams in red and green
Had ne'er before upon the boards of Yankeedom been seen;
And my proud name was heralded,—oh that I'd gone incog.
When we took that play to Providence to try it on a dog!

Shall I forget the awful day we struck that wretched town?
Yet in what melting irony the treacherous sun beamed down!
The sale of seats had not been large; but then McCambridge said
The factory people seldom bought their seats so far ahead,
And Rae indorsed McCambridge. So they partly set at rest
The natural misgivings that perturbed my youthful breast;
For I wondered and lamented that the town was not agog
When I took my play to Providence to try it on a dog.

They never came at all,—aha! I knew it all the time,—
They never came to see and hear my tragedy sublime.
Oh, fateful moment when the curtain rose on act the first!
Oh, moment fateful to the soul for wealth and fame athirst!
But lucky factory girls and boys to stay away that night,
When the author's fervid soul was touched by disappointment's blight,—
When desolation settled down on me like some dense fog
For having tempted Providence, and tried it on a dog!

Those actors didn't know their parts; they maundered to and fro,
Ejaculating platitudes that were quite mal à propos;
And when I sought to reprimand the graceless scamps, the lot
Turned fiercely on me, and denounced my charming play as rot.
I might have stood their bitter taunts without a passing grunt,
If I'd had a word of solace from the people out in front;
But that chilly corporal's guard sat round like bumps upon a log
When I played that play at Providence with designs upon the dog.

We went with lots of baggage, but we didn't bring it back,—
For who would be so hampered as he walks a railway track?
"Oh, ruthless muse of tragedy! what prodigies of shame,
What marvels of injustice are committed in thy name!"
Thus groaned I in the spirit, as I strode what stretch of ties
'Twixt Providence, Rhode Island, and my native Gotham lies;
But Rae, McCambridge, and the rest kept up a steady jog,—
'Twas not the first time they had plied their arts upon the dog.

So much for my first battle with the fickle goddess, Fame,—
And I hear that some folks nowadays are faring just the same.
Oh, hapless he that on the graceless Yankee dog relies!
The dog fares stout and hearty, and the play it is that dies.
So ye with tragedies to try, I beg of you, beware!
Put not your trust in Providence, that most delusive snare;

Cast, if you will, your pearls of thought before the Western hog,
But never go to Providence to try it on a dog.

GETTIN' ON

When I wuz somewhat younger,
I wuz reckoned purty gay;
I had my fling at everything
In a rollickin', coltish way.
But times have strangely altered
Since sixty years ago—
This age of steam an' things don't seem
Like the age I used to know.
Your modern innovations
Don't suit me, I confess,
As did the ways of the good ol' days,—
But I'm gettin' on, I guess.

I set on the piazza,
An' hitch round with the sun;
Sometimes, mayhap, I take a nap,
Waitin' till school is done.
An' then I tell the children
The things I done in youth,—
An' near as I can, as a vener'ble man,
I stick to the honest truth,—
But the looks of them 'at listen
Seem sometimes to express
The remote idee that I'm gone—you see?—
An' I am gettin' on, I guess.

I get up in the mornin',
An', nothin' else to do,
Before the rest are up an' dressed,
I read the papers through.
I hang round with the women
All day an' hear 'em talk;
An' while they sew or knit I show
The baby how to walk.
An', somehow, I feel sorry
When they put away his dress
An' cut his curls ('cause they're like a girl's!)—
I'm gettin' on, I guess.

Sometimes, with twilight round me,
I see, or seem to see,
A distant shore where friends of yore
Linger an' watch for me.
Sometimes I've heered 'em callin'

So tender-like 'nd low
That it almost seemed like a dream I dreamed,
Or an echo of long ago;
An' sometimes on my forehead
There falls a soft caress,
Or the touch of a hand,—you understand,—
I'm gettin' on, I guess.

THE SCHNELLEST ZUG

From Hanover to Leipzig is but a little way,
Yet the journey by the so-called schnellest zug consumes a day;
You start at half-past ten or so, and not till nearly night
Do the double towers of Magdeburg loom up before your sight;
From thence to Leipzig 's quick enough,—of that I'll not complain,—
But from Hanover to Magdeburg—confound that schnellest train!

The Germans say that "schnell" means fast, and "schnellest" faster yet,—
In all my life no grimmer bit of humor have I met!
Why, thirteen miles an hour 's the greatest speed they ever go,
While on the engine piston-rods do moss and lichens grow;
And yet the average Teuton will presumptuously maintain
That one can't know what swiftness is till he's tried das schnellest train!

Fool that I was! I should have walked,—I had no time to waste;
The little journey I had planned I had to do in haste,—
The quaint old town of Leipzig with its literary mart,
And Dresden with its crockery-shops and wondrous wealth of art,
The Saxon Alps, the Carlsbad cure for all dyspeptic pain,—
These were the ends I had in view when I took that schnellest train.

The natives dozed around me, yet none too deep to hear
The guard's sporadic shout of "funf minuten" (meaning beer);
I counted forty times at least that voice announce the stops
Required of those fat natives to glut their greed for hops,
Whilst I crouched in a corner, a monument to woe,
And thought unholy, awful things, and felt my whiskers grow!
And then, the wretched sights one sees while travelling by that train,—
The women doing men-folks' work at harvesting the grain,
Or sometimes grubbing in the soil, or hitched to heavy carts
Beside the family cow or dog, doing their slavish parts!
The husbands strut in soldier garb,—indeed they were too vain
To let creation see them work from that creeping schnellest train!

I found the German language all too feeble to convey
The sentiments that surged through my dyspeptic hulk that day;
I had recourse to English, and exploded without stint
Such virile Anglo-Saxon as would never do in print,
But which assuaged my rising gorge and cooled my seething brain

While snailing on to Magdeburg upon that schnellest train.

The typical New England freight that maunders to and fro,
The upper Mississippi boats, the bumptious B. & O.,
The creeping Southern railroads with their other creeping things,
The Philadelphy cable that is run out West for rings,
The Piccadilly 'buses with their constant roll and shake,—
All have I tried, and yet I'd give the "schnellest zug" the cake!
My countrymen, if ever you should seek the German clime,
Put not your trust in Baedeker if you are pressed for time;
From Hanover to Magdeburg is many a weary mile
By "schnellest zug," but done afoot it seems a tiny while;
Walk, swim, or skate, and then the task will not appear in vain,
But you'll break the third commandment if you take the schnellest train!

BETHLEHEM-TOWN

As I was going to Bethlehem-town,
Upon the earth I cast me down
All underneath a little tree
That whispered in this wise to me:
"Oh, I shall stand on Calvary
And bear what burthen saveth thee!"

As up I fared to Bethlehem-town,
I met a shepherd coming down,
And thus he quoth: "A wondrous sight
Hath spread before mine eyes this night,—
An angel host most fair to see,
That sung full sweetly of a tree
That shall uplift on Calvary
What burthen saveth you and me!"

And as I gat to Bethlehem-town,
Lo! wise men came that bore a crown.
"Is there," cried I, "in Bethlehem
A King shall wear this diadem?"
"Good sooth," they quoth, "and it is He
That shall be lifted on the tree
And freely shed on Calvary
What blood redeemeth us and thee!"

Unto a Child in Bethlehem-town
The wise men came and brought the crown;
And while the infant smiling slept,
Upon their knees they fell and wept;
But, with her babe upon her knee,
Naught recked that Mother of the tree,
That should uplift on Calvary

What burthen saveth all and me.

Again I walk in Bethlehem-town
And think on Him that wears the crown.
I may not kiss His feet again,
Nor worship Him as did I then;
My King hath died upon the tree,
And hath outpoured on Calvary
What blood redeemeth you and me!

THE PEACE OF CHRISTMAS-TIME

Dearest, how hard it is to say
That all is for the best,
Since, sometimes, in a grievous way
God's will is manifest.

See with what hearty, noisy glee
Our little ones to-night
Dance round and round our Christmas-tree
With pretty toys bedight.

Dearest, one voice they may not hear,
One face they may not see,—
Ah, what of all this Christmas cheer
Cometh to you and me?

Cometh before our misty eyes
That other little face;
And we clasp, in tender, reverent wise,
That love in the old embrace.

Dearest, the Christ-Child walks to-night,
Bringing His peace to men;
And He bringeth to you and to me the light
Of the old, old years again:

Bringeth the peace of long ago
When a wee one clasped your knee
And lisped of the morrow,—dear one, you know,—
And here come back is he!

Dearest, 'tis sometimes hard to say
That all is for the best,
For, often in a grievous way,
God's will is manifest.

But in the grace of this holy night
That bringeth us back our child,

Let us see that the ways of God are right,
And so be reconciled.

THE DOINGS OF DELSARTE

In former times my numerous rhymes excited general mirth,
And I was then of all good men the merriest man on earth;
And my career
From year to year
Was full of cheer
And things,
Despite a few regrets, perdieu! which grim dyspepsia brings;
But now how strange and harsh a change has come upon the scene!
Horrors appall the life where all was formerly so serene:
Yes, wasting care hath cast its snare about my honest heart,
Because, alas! it hath come to pass my daughter's learned Delsarte.
In flesh and joint and every point the counterpart of me,
She grew so fast she grew at last a marvellous thing to see,—
Long, gaunt, and slim, each gangling limb played stumbling-block to t'other,
The which excess of awkwardness quite mortified her mother.
Now, as for me, I like to see the carriages uncouth
Which certify to all the shy, unconscious age of youth.
If maidenkind be pure of mind, industrious, tidy, smart,
What need that they should fool away their youth upon Delsarte?

In good old times my numerous rhymes occasioned general mirth,
But now you see
Revealed in me
The gloomiest bard on earth.
I sing no more of the joys of yore that marked my happy life,
But rather those depressing woes with which the present's rife.
Unreconciled to that gaunt child, who's now a fashion-plate,
One song I raise in Art's dispraise, and so do I fight with Fate:
This gangling bard has found it hard to see his counterpart
Long, loose, and slim, divorced from him by that hectic dude,
Delsarte.

Where'er she goes,
She loves to pose,
In classic attitudes,
And droop her eyes in languid wise, and feign abstracted moods;
And she, my child,
Who all so wild,
So helpless and so sweet,
That once she knew not what to do with those great big hands and feet,
Now comes and goes with such repose, so calmly sits or stands,
Is so discreet with both her feet, so deft with both her hands.
Why, when I see that satire on me, I give an angry start,
And I utter one word—it is commonly heard—derogatory to Delsarte.

In years gone by 't was said that I was quite a scrumptious man;
Conceit galore had I before this Delsarte craze began;
But now these wise
Folks criticise
My figure and my face,
And I opine they even incline to sneer at my musical bass.
Why, sometimes they presume to say this wart upon my cheek
Is not refined, and remarks unkind they pass on that antique,—
With lusty bass and charms of face and figure will I part
Ere they extort this grand old wart to placat their Delsarte.

Oh, wretched day! as all shall say who've known my Muse before,
When by this rhyme you see that I'm not in it any more.
Good-by the mirth that over earth diffused such keen delight;
The old-time bard
Of pork and lard
Is plainly out of sight.
All withered now about his brow the laurel fillets droop,
While Lachesis brews
For the poor old Muse
A portion of scalding soup.
Engrave this line, O friends of mine! over my broken heart:
"He hustled and strove, and fancied he throve, till his daughter
learned Delsarte."

BUTTERCUP, POPPY, FORGET-ME-NOT

Buttercup, Poppy, Forget-me-not,—
These three bloomed in a garden spot;
And once, all merry with song and play,
A little one heard three voices say:
"Shine or shadow, summer or spring,
O thou child with the tangled hair
And laughing eyes, we three shall bring
Each an offering, passing fair!"
The little one did not understand;
But they bent and kissed the dimpled hand.

Buttercup gambolled all day long,
Sharing the little one's mirth and song;
Then, stealing along on misty gleams,
Poppy came, bringing the sweetest dreams,
Playing and dreaming, that was all,
Till once the sleeper would not awake;
Kissing the little face under the pall,
We thought of the words the third flower spake,
And we found, betimes, in a hallowed spot,
The solace and peace of Forget-me-not.

Buttercup shareth the joy of day,
Glinting with gold the hours of play;
Bringeth the Poppy sweet repose,
When the hands would fold and the eyes would close.
And after it all,—the play and the sleep
Of a little life,—what cometh then?
To the hearts that ache and the eyes that weep,
A wee flower bringeth God's peace again:
Each one serveth its tender lot,—
Buttercup, Poppy, Forget-me-not.

Eugene Field – A Short Biography

Eugene Field was born on 2nd September, 1850 in St. Louis, Missouri at 634 S. Broadway to parents Roswell Martin and Frances Reed Field, both of New England stock. Tragically Field lost his mother at age 6 and was thereafter brought up by a cousin, Mary Field French, in Amherst, Massachusetts.

Field attended Williams College in Williamstown, Massachusetts.

When he was 19 his father died, and Field dropped out of Williams. Field's father, Roswell Martin Field, was the lawyer for Dred Scott, the slave who famously sued for his freedom. The complaint was sometimes referred to as 'The lawsuit that started the Civil War'.

Field then went to Knox College in Galesburg, Illinois, but again dropped out. This time after a year. However he did then summon himself to attend the University of Missouri in Columbia, Missouri, where his brother Roswell was studying. As can be gathered from his efforts to date Field was not the most serious of students but was gaining the reputation of being a prankster. Among his more outlandish attempts were a raid on the president's wine cellar, painting the president's house in school colors, and firing the school's landmark cannons at midnight.

Field tried acting but found it not to his liking, studied law but with little success, but did have an interest in writing for the student newspaper.

When his studies finished in 1871, although he never graduated, he collected his share of his inheritance from his father's estate, and set off for a trip to explore Europe. After six months, with funds from the inheritance exhausted, he returned to the United States.

Field then set to work as a journalist for the St. Joseph Gazette in Saint Joseph, Missouri, in 1875.

That same year he married the sixteen-year-old Julia Sutherland Comstock of St Joseph, Missouri. They would eventually have eight children during their twenty-two years of marriage, of whom only five would reach adulthood. Field, knowing that his understanding of finances was somewhat poor, arranged for all the money he earned to be sent to his wife for her to administer on behalf of the family.

In his career as a journalist he soon found a niche that suited him. His articles were light, humorous and written in a personal and gossipy style that endeared him to his readership. Some were soon being syndicated to other newspapers around the States. Field rose to be the city editor of the Gazette.

From 1876 through 1880, the Family lived in St. Louis. Field worked initially as an editorial writer for the Morning Journal and then for the Times-Journal. From there he worked for a short time as the managing editor of the Kansas City Times before settling, for two years, as the editor of the Denver Tribune. He also wrote a column for the paper, 'Odds and Ends,' poking fun at the climate, the muddy roads, the frontier language, and other aspects of Denver life. However his readership was large and growing. Further opportunities would come.

In 1883 the Field moved the family to Chicago lured by a salary of $50 a week. Field now began work for the Chicago Daily News. Here he wrote his humorous newspaper column called Sharps and Flats. He quickly found out that $50 dollars in Denver didn't stretch that far in bustling Chicago.

His column ran in the newspaper's morning edition. In it Field made quips about issues and personalities of the day, especially regarding the arts and literature. His pet subject was the intellectual superiority of Chicago, especially when he compared it to Boston, which he often did. In April 1887, he wrote, "While Chicago is humping herself in the interests of literature, art and the sciences, vain old Boston is frivoling away her precious time in an attempted renaissance of the cod fisheries."

In another article that year after Chicago's National League baseball club sold future baseball Hall of Famer Mike "King" Kelly to Boston which overlapped with a speaking tour visit from the famous Boston poet and diplomat James Russell Lowell he wrote: "Chicago feels a special interest in Mr. Lowell at this particular time because he is perhaps the foremost representative of the enterprising and opulent community which within the last week has secured the services of one of Chicago's honored sons for the base-ball season of 1887. The fact that Boston has come to Chicago for the captain of her baseball nine has reinvigorated the bonds of affection between the metropolis of the Bay state and the metropolis of the mighty west; the truth of this will appear in the mighty welcome which our public will give Mr. Lowell next Tuesday."

It was in 1888 that his poem 'Little Boy Blue' was printed in America, a weekly journal. It achieved for Field instant and lasting fame. Coincidentally the same issue carried a poem by James Russell Lowell. Field was immensely pleased that his own poem was regarded with considerably more weight and acclaim.

Field had first published poetry in 1879, when his poem 'Christmas Treasures' was published. It later appeared in 'A Little Book of Western Verse' (1889). This was the beginning that would eventually number over a dozen volumes. He developed a style of light-hearted poems for children. Among the perennial favorites are 'Wynken, Blynken, and Nod' and 'The Duel' (but better known as 'The Gingham Dog and the Calico Cat') and 'Little Boy Blue' about the death of a child. As well as verse Field published an extensive range of short stories including 'The Holy Cross' and 'Daniel and the Devil.'

Field treasured rare, unusual and beautiful books and his personal library had scores of them. He also enjoyed making them too and frequently worked long hours with great care and various colored inks decorating the first letter of his poems.

In 1889 whilst the family were in London and Field himself was recovering from a bout of ill health he wrote his most famous poem; 'Lovers Lane'. It is often thought to have been written whilst the couple were courting but recent research settles it authorship to this later date. The poem was written as a reminder of better days when the couple courted in her father's buggy on 'Lover's Lane, St Jo'.

Field was ever curious and keen to push his boundaries. In 1891 with his brother Roswell they wrote and published 'Echoes from the Sabine Farm' a loosely translated version of Horace.

On 4th November 1895 Eugene Field Sr died in Chicago of a heart attack at the age of 45. He is buried at the Church of the Holy Comforter in Kenilworth, Illinois.

The New York Times described his death: CHICAGO, Nov. 4. — Eugene Field, the poet and humorist, died at 5 o'clock this morning of heart disease at his residence in Buena Park. Although Mr. Field had been ill for the past three days, his sudden death was totally unexpected.

Field was originally interred at Graceland Cemetery in Chicago, but his son-in-law, Senior Warden of the Church of the Holy Comforter, had him reinterred on 7th March, 1926.

Several of his poems were set to music with commercial success. Many of his works were accompanied by paintings from the exceptional talents of Maxfield Parrish.

During his lifetime he was often referred to as the 'poet of childhood'. This may account for his anonymous publication of 'Only a Boy'. In our own times the work would probably be frowned upon. It concerns a 12-year-old boy being seduced by a woman in her 30s. The 1920's drama critic/magazine editor George Jean Nathan claimed it was a popular but forbidden work among those coming of age in the early 1900's.

Much of what Field wrote was light, humourous and of its time. And that is perhaps why it has endured. Its writes of a time that, in his words, suspends itself from the harsh reality of real life to a gentler and more touching time that exists in the imagination.

Eugene Field – A Concise Bibliography

The Tribune Primer (1882)
Culture's Garland (1887)
A Little Book of Profitable Tales (1889)
A Little Book of Western Verse (1889)
With Trumpet and Drum (1892)
Echoes from the Sabine Farm (1893)
The Holy Cross and Other Tales (1893)
Second Book of Verse (1893)
Love Songs of Childhood (1894)
Love Affairs of a Bibliomaniac (1895)
Little Willie (1895)
Songs and Other Verse (1896)
Second Book of Tales (1896)
The House; An Episode in the Lives of Reuben Baker, Astronomer and His Wife Alice (1896)
Field Flowers (1896)
Florence Bardsley's Story (1897)
Lullaby Songs of Childhood (1897)
Lullaby Land (1898)

Sharps and Flats (1900)
The Stars (1901)
Nonsense for Old and Young (1901)
A Little Book of Nonsense (1901)
A Little Book of Tribune Verse (1901)
The Sabine Farm (1903)
John Smith USA (1905)
The Clink of Ice (1905)
Hoosier Lyrics (1905)
Cradle Lullabies (1909)
The Poems of Eugene Field (1910)
Christmas Tales and Christmas Verse (1912)
Penn-Yan Bill's Wooing (1914)
The Yankee Abroad (1917)
The Mouse and the Moonbeam (1919)
Poems of Childhood (1920)
The Gingham Dog and the Calico Cat (1926)
Child Verses (1927)
The Sugar Plum Tree (1929)
In Wink-a-way Land (1930)

www.ingramcontent.com/pod-product-compliance
Lightning Source LLC
Chambersburg PA
CBHW060136050426
42448CB00010B/2153